Collins Illustrated Guide to
GUILIN, CANTON AND GUANGDONG

COLLINS

8 Grafton Street, London W1
1988

William Collins Sons & Co. Ltd
London • Glasgow • Sydney • Auckland
Toronto • Johannesburg

British Library Cataloguing in Publication Data

Collins Illustrated Guide to Guilin, Canton and Guangdong — (China Guides Series)
1. Guilin (China) — Description and Travel — Guide-books
I. Series
915.1'27   DS796.C2

ISBN 0-00-215266-5

First published 1988
Copyright © The Guidebook Company Ltd 1988

Series Editors: May Holdsworth and Jill Hunt
Picture Editor: Ingrid Morejohn

Text by Paddy Booz, Chang Tsong-zung, Shann Davies (173−88), Katherine Forestier, Simon Holledge, Jill Hunt, Anthony Lawrence (44−7), Diana Martin (148−9) and Harry Rolnick (58−69)

Photographs by The Guidebook Company Limited, with additional contributions by Chang Tsong-zung (7 top right, 145); Katherine Forestier (6, 7 bottom right, 149, 194−5); Jardine, Matheson and Co Limited (93); James Montgomery (38−9 and cover) and Ingrid Morejohn (7 left)

Design by Joan Law Design & Photography

Printed in Hong Kong

Contents

Yao mother and child, northern Guangdong

Street-stall wares in Guilin

Lianxian County, northern Guangdong

Special Topics

Maps

All prices in this book refer to 1987 and are included for comparative purposes.

Names and Addresses

In this book addresses are given in *Pinyin*. *Dajie*, *Dalu* and *Dadao* are main thoroughfares; *lu* is a road and *jie* is a street; *xiang* is a lane or alley.

To help visitors getting about on their own, names of hotels and restaurants are given in Chinese characters in the text, while names of all the sights and other places described in the book are given in Chinese characters either in the Useful Addresses section or in the Index of Places.

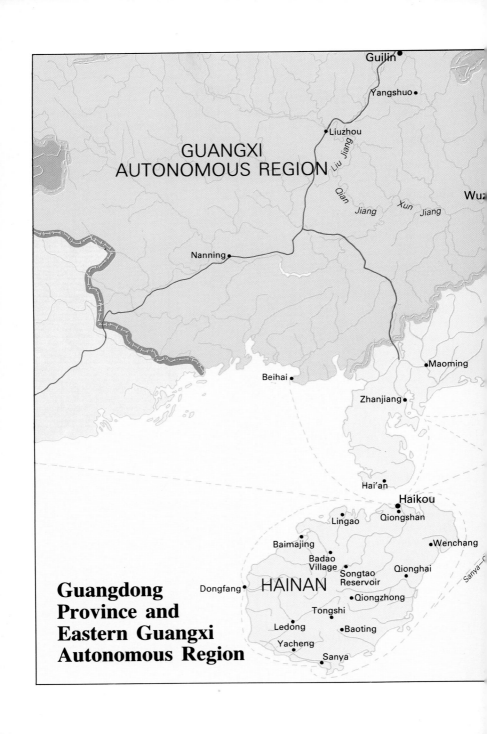

Guilin

Yangshuo•

Liuzhou•

GUANGXI
AUTONOMOUS REGION

Liu Jiang

Qian Jiang *Xun Jiang*

Wuz

Nanning•

Maoming

Beihai•

Zhanjiang•

Hai'an•

Haikou

•Lingao Qiongshan

Baimajing• •Wenchang

Badao
Village• Qionghai

Songtao
Reservoir Qionghai

Sanya-C

Dongfang• HAINAN

•Qiongzhong

Tongshi•

**Guangdong
Province and
Eastern Guangxi
Autonomous Region**

Ledong• •Baoting

Yacheng•

Sanya•

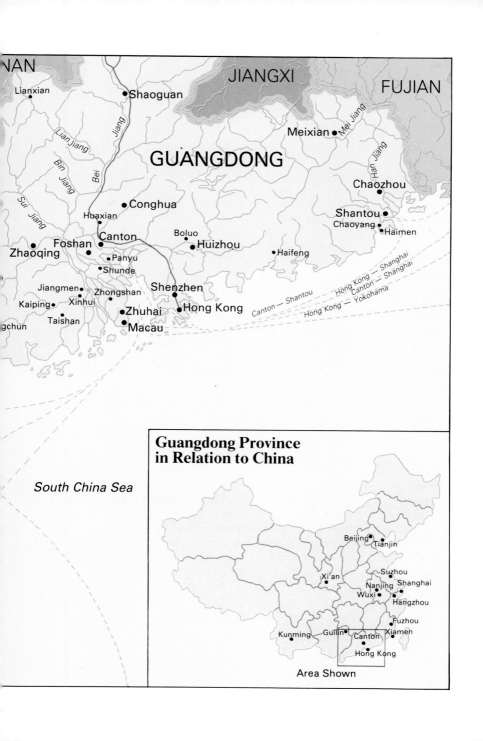

General Information for Travellers

Climate and Clothing

Canton has a subtropical climate. The best season to visit is the autumn when humidity is relatively low, skies are sunny and daytime temperatures hover around 22°C (70°F) with slightly cooler evenings. The least pleasant time is between late January and April, with frequent rain and chilly weather. Summertime is hot and humid with temperatures often above 33°C (90°F). From mid July to the end of October is the typhoon season, when great swirling storms can arise in the South China Sea and smash into the mainland. If a major typhoon strikes, as they do every three or four years, travel plans can be upset for several days.

Cotton and cotton-synthetic clothes are the most comfortable throughout the year. In winter, light woollen suits and overcoats are recommended. Tourists rarely need formal wear, but business travellers should bring appropriate clothes for formal meetings and banquets. Diners at Canton's more expensive Western restaurants tend to be smartly dressed. Reasonably-styled Chinese-made clothes (especially sweaters, shirts, and synthetic jackets) may be bought in Canton.

The climate of Canton can be applied generally to the entire province of Guangdong. The mountains in the north and east are colder in winter while the Leizhou Peninsula and Hainan Island remain warm throughout the year.

Although geographically part of southern China, Guilin's climate is generally thought to be more pleasant than Canton's, even though the summer months can be just as hot and humid as in much of Guangdong Province. The best time to visit Guilin is autumn and early winter, when it is relatively cool and dry. January and February tend to be cold and cloudy, and woollens and a jacket are necessary. In spring and summer rainfall is most frequent; almost half of Guilin's average annual rainfall occurring in May and June. Light cottons and rain gear are advisable for the summer months (May-September).

Average Temperatures in Guilin °C (°F)

	Average	High	Low		Average	High	Low
Jan	8 (46)	13 (56)	5 (41)	Jul	28 (82)	34 (94)	24 (75)
Feb	9 (48)	13 (56)	6 (42)	Aug	28 (82)	34 (94)	24 (74)
Mar	13 (56)	17 (62)	10 (50)	Sept	26 (78)	33 (93)	21 (70)
Apr	18 (65)	24 (75)	15 (58)	Oct	21 (69)	28 (82)	17 (62)
May	23 (74)	29 (84)	20 (67)	Nov	15 (59)	21 (69)	11 (51)
Jun	26 (79)	32 (89)	22 (72)	Dec	10 (50)	16 (62)	6 (43)

Average Temperatures in Canton °C (°F)

	Average	High	Low		Average	High	Low
Jan	14 (57)	28 (82)	1 (33)	Jul	28 (83)	39 (99)	22 (71)
Feb	15 (58)	29 (84)	0 (32)	Aug	28 (83)	39 (102)	22 (72)
Mar	18 (64)	31 (88)	4 (39)	Sept	27 (81)	36 (97)	18 (65)
Apr	22 (71)	33 (91)	11 (50)	Oct	24 (75)	33 (92)	11 (52)
May	26 (78)	36 (96)	15 (60)	Nov	20 (67)	32 (89)	5 (42)
Jun	27 (81)	35 (95)	20 (68)	Dec	15 (59)	28 (83)	2 (36)

Visas

Everyone must get a visa to go to China, but this is usually an easy, trouble-free process. Tourists travelling in a group are listed on a single group visa — a special document listing all members of the group — which is issued in advance to tour organizers. Individual passports of people travelling on a group visa will not be stamped unless specifically requested.

Tourist visas for individual travellers (those who are not travelling in a group) can be obtained directly through Chinese embassies and consulates, although some embassies are more enthusiastic about issuing them than others. Certain travel agents and tour operators around the world can arrange individual visas for their clients. It is simplest in Hong Kong, where there are a large number of travel agents handling visa applications. Just one passport photograph and a completed application form are necessary.

Visa fees vary considerably, depending on the source of the visa, and on the time taken to get it. In Hong Kong, for instance, some travel agents can get you a tourist visa in a few hours, but it may cost around US$30 for one valid for three months, while a one-month visa which takes 48 hours to obtain might cost just US$6.50.

The visa gives you automatic entry to all China's open cities and areas (there were 436 in 1987).

The mechanics of getting a business visa are much more flexible than in the past, particularly in Hong Kong. The applicant should have either an invitation from the appropriate Foreign Trade Corporation (several now have permanent representatives abroad), or from the organizers of a specialized trade fair or seminar. In Hong Kong, all that is needed is a letter from the applicant's company confirming that he wishes to travel to China on business.

Regular business visitors are eligible for a multiple re-entry visa which may be obtained with the help of a business contact in China. Some Hong Kong travel agents can also arrange re-entry visas for clients — the cost might be around US$50−60. This type of visa may be for three or six months.

Customs

A customs declaration form must be filled out by each visitor upon entry. On this document you are required to list valuable personal possessions such as tape recorders, cameras, watches, jewellery etc, as well as foreign currency. The carbon copy of this form will be returned to you and it must be produced at customs for inspection on departure from China.

Any antique bought for export should bear a brown or red wax seal, which tells customs officials that it may be taken out of the country, so be sure to keep the seal on. It is also advisable to keep all sales receipts.

Four bottles of alcohol, three cartons of cigarettes, unlimited film and unlimited medicines for personal use may be taken in. Firearms and dangerous drugs are strictly forbidden. It is also illegal to acquire Chinese money abroad and take it in.

Money

Chinese Currency The Chinese currency, which is sometimes referred to as Renminbi or Rmb, meaning 'people's currency', is denominated in *yuan* which are each divided into 10 *jiao*, colloquially called *mao*. Each *jiao* is, in turn, divided into 10 *fen*. There are large notes for 100, 50, 10, 5, 2 and 1 *yuan*, small notes for 5, 2 and 1 *jiao*, and coins for 5, 2 and 1 *fen*.

Currency Certificates Foreign Exchange Certificates (FEC) were introduced in 1980. They were designed to be used instead of Renminbi by foreign visitors for payment in hotels, Friendship Stores, at trade fairs, and for airline tickets, international phone calls, parcel post etc. In practice, however, FEC quickly became a sought-after form of payment anywhere, and a black market developed between the two currencies. In September 1986 the Chinese government announced its intention of phasing out FECs, but implementation seems to have been indefinitely postponed, and FECs remain in circulation.

FEC and Rmb may be reconverted into foreign currency or taken out when you leave China, but it is impossible to change them abroad.

Foreign Currency There is no limit to the amount of foreign currency you can bring into China. It is advisable to keep your exchange vouchers as the bank may demand to see them when you convert Chinese currency back into foreign currency on leaving China.

Cheques and Credit Cards All the usual American, European and Japanese travellers cheques are acceptable. Credit cards may be used in a limited number of Friendship Stores, hotels and banks, and you should check with your credit card company or bank before you rely on this form of payment for your purchases.

Tipping Although China's tourism authorities say that tipping is forbidden, the practice has made a reappearance. Taxi drivers and some other personnel working in the travel industry have been accepting tips for some time.

Travel Agencies

There are a number of State-owned corporations which handle foreign visitors to China, but the largest is China International Travel Service (CITS). Other large organizations providing similar services are China Travel Service (CTS) and China Youth Travel Service (CYTS).

CITS offers a comprehensive service covering accommodation, transport, food, sightseeing, interpreters and special visits to schools, hospitals, factories and other places foreigners might be interested to see. It also provides services such as ticket sales for walk-in customers. See pages 200–204 for addresses of CITS and CTS offices in the province.

Over the past few years a number of new travel agencies, offering city tours or handling travel to other parts of the province, have opened. Some are privately owned, and others are run by collectives or by corporations. Standards of service offered vary considerably.

Communications

Facilities for long-distance calls from Guangdong, and the nearby Special Economic Zones, are amongst the best in China. IDD (International Direct Dialling) is available in 13 cities — Canton, Dongguan, Foshan, Haikou, Jiangmen, Shantou, Shekou, Shenzhen, Shunde, Zhanjiang, Zhaoqing, Zhongshan and Zhuhai. Hong Kong, Macau and 13 other overseas countries, as well as 45 cities within China, can be reached by IDD. But it can still be a time-consuming process to make long-distance and international calls through the operator, since the system is heavily overstretched. Most hotels will place calls for you.

The number of telex and facsimile installations in the region is rapidly increasing and telex is available in most middle-range hotels.

Because of the proximity to Hong Kong, a number of foreign English-language newspapers and magazines are for sale in the main hotels without too much of a time lag. China's own English-language newspaper *China Daily* can be found in many hotels throughout the region.

Holidays

In contrast to the long calendar of traditional Chinese festivals, modern China now has only three official holidays: May Day, 1 October (marking the founding of the People's Republic of China), and Chinese New Year, usually called the Spring Festival in China itself, which comes at the lunar new year.

Guilin

Guilin, or Kweilin as it used to be spelt, is arguably China's most famous beauty spot. The astonishing scenery that surrounds this small city has been celebrated for many hundreds of years on Chinese scrolls and in poetry. Not surprisingly, the images inspired by Guilin, with its craggy peaks partly shrouded in mist, have been a powerful basis for the Western stereotype of Chinese landscape.

Chinese poets and artists over the centuries have stressed that Guilin's limestone mountains, sculpted by wind and rain into fantastic shapes, have to be seen to be believed.

'I often sent pictures of the hills of Guilin which I painted to friends back home', commented the Song-Dynasty writer Fan Chengda, 'but few believed what they saw. There is no point in arguing with them.'

The scenery has proved compelling to artists in many different eras. The Tang poet Han Yu described the strange rock hills as 'blue jade hairpins', while Liu Zongyuan said 'they rise abruptly from the earth like trees in a forest'. Another poet Liu Shuzhi saw the area as an imaginary sea, with strangely-shaped rocks floating around the city.

Chinese writers have found Guilin's caves equally strange and interesting. Wrote Luo Dajing in 1784:

Seeing the blue hills from the outside
Is like touching the exterior of a person
Seeing the hills from inside the caverns
Is like plucking his internal organs.

Today, tourists continue to pour into the city to marvel at the mountains and caves, and to make the famous boat trip from Guilin to Yangshuo. The scenery attracts 350,000 or so overseas visitors each year, and many more domestic tourists who regard Guilin as the ideal destination for a romantic holiday or a honeymoon.

Guilin's popularity at home and overseas inevitably has resulted in a rush of hotel building, a rise in prices, and an ever increasing number of souvenir hawkers, along with aggressive money-changers, and restauranteurs trying to lure passers-by into their establishments.

As a town, Guilin is pleasant enough, but has little of real historical significance. Until the Qin it was a small village of no importance. But in 214 BC the Ling Canal was completed (see page 37), linking the Pearl and Yangzi River networks, and Guilin became established as a regional trading centre. During the Ming Dynasty it grew in importance, becoming capital of Guangxi Province, a title which it held until 1914.

In 1936, Nationalist armies — driven back by the Japanese from the coast — fled to Guilin which they briefly made their capital before

Guilin

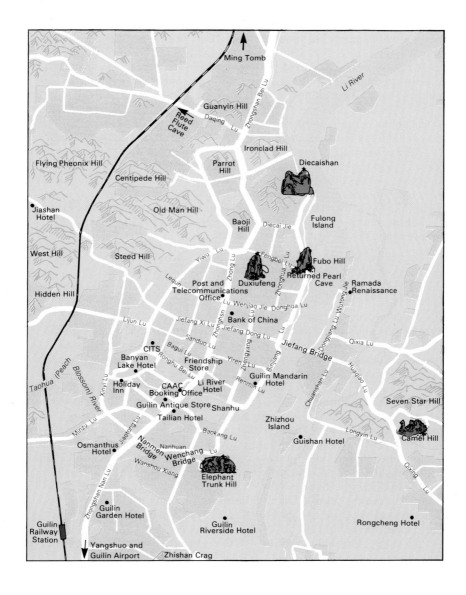

Ming Tomb

Li River

Guanyin Hill

Reed Flute Cave

Daqing Lu

Zhongshan Bei Lu

Ironclad Hill

Flying Pheonix Hill

Parrot Hill

Diecaishan

Centipede Hill

Jiashan Hotel

Old Man Hill

Baoji Hill

Diecai Jie

Fulong Island

West Hill

Steed Hill

Yiwu Lu

Fengbei Lu

Zhong Lu

Fubo Hill

Duxiufeng

Zhonghua

Returned Pearl Cave

Ramada Renaissance

Hidden Hill

Lequn

Post and Telecommunications Office

Lu Wenjiao Jie

Donghua Lu

Wutong Jie

Lijun Lu

Jiefang Xi Lu

Bank of China

Zhongshan

Jiefang Dong Lu

Donglang Lu

Sanduo Lu

Zhengyang

Jiefang Bridge

Huagiao Lu

Qixia Lu

CITS

Bagui Lu

Banyan Lake Hotel

Ronghu Bei Lu

Yiren Lu

Friendship Store

Binjiang

Chuansham Lu

Holiday Inn

Xinyi Lu

CAAC Booking Office

Li River Hotel

Zhengyang Lu

Renmin Lu

Guilin Mandarin Hotel

Seven Star Hill

Guilin Antique Store

Shanhu

Taihua (Peach Blossom) River

Taihua (Peach

Blossom) River

Tailian Hotel

Zhizhou Island

Longyin Lu

Camel Hill

Osmanthus Hotel

Minzu Lu

Jiaotong Lu

Nanmen Bridge

Nanhuan

Baokang Lu

Guishan Hotel

Qixing Lu

Wenchang Bridge

Lu

Wanshou Xiang

Elephant Trunk Hill

Zhongshan Nan Lu

Guilin Garden Hotel

Guilin Riverside Hotel

Rongcheng Hotel

Guilin Railway Station

Yangshuo and Guilin Airport

Zhishan Crag

moving on to Chongqing. For a short period a flood of affluent Chinese families converged on Guilin, swelling the population to over a million people.

A sudden Japanese offensive routed the unprepared Nationalist forces in 1944 and Guilin fell to the Japanese who captured a large cache of unused weapons. In a spree of destruction, Japanese armies wiped out much of the town and, with it, most of the evidence of the region's history.

The modern city of Guilin, which has grown up over the last 35 years, has little of its former charm and elegance. But recently more conscious steps have been taken to improve the environment. Some of the factories responsible for polluting the area have been moved away, and the central government has provided 'beautification' funding for the city. Lakes have been dredged and cleaned up, and roads rebuilt, so that Guilin is now a pleasant place to walk or cycle.

The new hotels have helped raise not just the poor quality of accommodation, but also the standard of food in Guilin, which has never been noted for its culinary excellence. Many of the joint-venture hotels have imported chefs from Hong Kong, and have also introduced into Guilin the first real Western restaurants.

Small restaurants have sprung up to cater to the overseas visitors — some of them advertising Western dishes. The quality of home-cooking in some of these tiny establishments is excellent, although surroundings can be very basic. The main feature of Guilin's food is its use of wild game — civet cat, scaly pangolin (an endangered species), owl, lynx, turtle, flying fruit bat — and these dishes can be requested in many of the local restaurants.

Getting to Guilin

By Air There are direct flights from Hong Kong on new Hong Kong-based carrier Dragonair four times a week (US$82). CAAC has one or two flights each day from Hong Kong departing early evening. Guilin has air links with most major cities in China, and there are four or five flights a day from Canton (Rmb273).

By Road Several buses depart daily for Guilin from Wuzhou, a town on the border of Guangdong Province and Guangxi Autonomous region (Rmb18). A hovercraft to Wuzhou leaves from Hong Kong early in the morning on alternate days, travelling up the Pearl River (Zhujiang) into its main estaury (Xijiang) and arriving in Wuzhou 11 hours later (Rmb125). The two-day bus-ride to Guilin from Canton is only recommended for travellers who specialize in bus travel.

By Train Rail links with other cities are not particularly practical. The train from Canton to Guilin takes 17 hours and goes via the city of Hengyang in Hunan Province, a major rail junction. From Kunming to Guilin it is a 24-hour trip and the journey to Beijing takes 58 hours.

Getting around Guilin

Taxis are available at the main hotels but, with the rapid increase in foreign visitors, are in short supply. You can hire a trishaw for shorter journeys, although settling a reasonable price may turn out to be a lengthy process. Motorized trishaws also cruise the streets, and will travel longer distances.

Bicycling is an excellent way to see Guilin. Roads are flat, and, aside from the crowded Zhongshan Lu and Jiefang Bridge, not very busy. There are a number of small bicycle-hire shops along Zhongshan Lu. Costs vary depending upon how hard you bargain, but asking price in 1987 was around Rmb10 a day. It is possible to reach all the main hills and caves in the city (where you just lock up and leave the bicycle along with the hundreds of others already parked there). Without much effort you can cycle out into the surrounding countryside and onto the dirt tracks that wind through the superb landscape of craggy hills.

City tours are offered by many small companies located near the train station and on Zhongshan Lu. The La La Café, Dasanyuan Restaurant, and Nanyuan Restaurant all arrange special tours to various areas around Guilin which are difficult for an individual to get to. Groups are usually small and prices reasonable.

Hotels in Guilin

Guilin was once notorious for the dismal quality of its hotels, but its reputation is rapidly changing with the construction of a number of new joint-venture hotels, managed by foreign hotel groups. The city's older hotels have also tried to upgrade their facilities and improve services with the result that the visitor now has a wide choice of accommodation with varying prices.

Superior

Guilin Mandarin
Binjiang Nan Lu
tel. 5713 tlx. 48339

Double rooms US$80, suites US$100

Due to open in 1988, the 392-room Guilin Mandarin (no relation to the Mandarin in

桂林文华大饭店
滨江南路

Hong Kong) is well located, within the city and overlooking the river, directly opposite the pier for Li River cruise boats. Its facilities will include a health centre with sauna and whirlpool, banquet hall, small conference complex (where 140 can be seated theatre-style), business centre, disco, rooftop bar. Rooms, with imported furnishings and interiors, are a good size.

Guishan Hotel
Chuanshan Lu
tel. 4059
tlx. 48443

桂山大酒店
穿山路

Double rooms US$70−80, suites US$140−400

The largest of the new wave of international standard hotels, this is situated on a spacious, secluded site on the east banks of the Li River. Its 600 rooms are spread out in three low-rise Chinese-style blocks, divided by gardens. Run by New World Hotels of Hong Kong, the Guishan part-opened in 1987, and will be finished in 1988. A special access road has been built and a tributary of the Li has been diverted to bring the water lapping up against some of the hotel walls. Recreation facilities include Guilin's only bowling alley, a swimming pool and billiard room. There is a large Cantonese restaurant as well as Western ones, health centre, disco and business centre. It is about ten minutes' walk to Jiefang Bridge, which takes you across the Li River into the town centre.

Holiday Inn Guilin
14 Ronghu Nan Lu
tel. 3950
tlx. 48456

假日桂林宾馆
榕湖路14号

Double rooms US$80, 90

This friendly 259-room hotel has a pleasant location overlooking Ronghu (Banyan) Lake in a quiet part of town. The city centre is within easy reach by trishaw, bicycle, or on foot. The lake and its banks have recently been cleaned up as part of a 'beautification' scheme paid for by the central government. Facilities are straightforward but comfortable — Chinese and Western restaurants, a bar and small health club — and Holiday Inn's service puts the hotel into the top bracket of Guilin's hotels

Ronghu Bei Lu
tel. 3811
tlx. 48461

榕湖饭店
榕湖北路

**Guilin Garland Hotel
(Kaiyue Jiudian)**
Zhongshan Nan Lu
tel. 2510/2
tlx. 48438

凯悦酒店
中山南路

**Li River Hotel
(Lijiang Fandian)**
Shanhu Bei Lu
tel. 2881
tlx. 48470

漓江饭店
杉湖北路

Rongcheng Hotel
Sanlidian
tel. 2311
tlx. 48447

榕城饭店
三里店

Jiashan Hotel
Jianshan Cun
tel. 2986
tlx. 48456

甲山饭店
甲山村

warlord Bai Chongxi. Conversion to a hotel began in 1954. Building Number Five is the newest and best building. The Chinese food here has a good reputation, especially if you are after the more exotic dishes such as lynx meat, beaver, dog, turtle and flying fruit bat.

Double rooms Rmb123

This middle-quality 300-room hotel, near the train station, partially opened in mid-1987. Some Hong Kong Chinese are employed in senior managerial positions. Facilities include Chinese and Western restaurants, a banquet hall and shopping centre.

Double rooms Rmb75, 85

Over the past few years, the Li River has worked hard to change its reputation as one China's worst hotels for foreign tourists. Renovation work and improved management have helped, although the hotel still cannot match its foreign-run competitors. It is, however, well located, and top-floor rooms have wonderful views.

Double rooms Rmb73

This hotel was completed in 1983, entirely Chinese-built with a gratuitous attempt at traditional style. Rooms are not well maintained, but do have airconditioning and television. It is located rather far out of the city, to the east near Seven Star Park.

Double rooms Rmb100

Just north of Guilin, this 330-room motel-style hotel was constructed with the help of an Australian firm in 1980 entirely from imported, prefabricated pieces. Maintenance has been very poor, and service continues to be mediocre at best.

Tailian Hotel
Zhongshan Zhong Lu
tel. 3020
tlx. 48453

台联饭店
中山中路

Double rooms Rmb150

Set just off the busy Zhongshan Lu in the
town centre, this hotel was built by a
Taiwanese Friendship Association. Rooms are
a reasonable quality by China standards, and
the Chinese restaurant has a good reputation
both with foreigners and locals alike. The
Tailian has 80 rooms, and a second phase with
108 more rooms was under construction in
1987. It is planned to employ a few Hong
Kong Chinese for key departments.

Guilin's Topography

Millions of years ago, the area around Guilin was under the sea. The
earth's crust there was formed by layer upon layer of sediment, as can be
clearly seen in the surface texture of the rocks today. A shifting of the
earth's crust caused part of it to buckle, resulting in the formation of
plateaus and valleys. Over thousands of years, erosion has produced the
spectacularly shaped peaks in Guilin today.

This topography is a perfect example of tropical karst landscape. The
generic term *karst* derives from the Serbo-Croat word 'kars' meaning a
'bleak waterless place' which typifies the jagged crests, assymmetrical
peaks and isolated domes of the Dinaric Alps in Yugoslavia.

The features of karst landscapes are a result of solution weathering of
thick pure limestone over many thousands of years. The calcium
carbonate in the limestone is carried away in solution by rain water
acidified by the carbon dioxide in the atmosphere. The rain water seeps
through the surface of the rock and forms underground streams and
rivers which produce the caves and caverns that are another feature of
this type of landscape.

It is the collapse of these underground caverns which helps to
produce the deep ravines and almost perpendicular slopes of karst
scenery which in Guilin is accentuated by the increased humidity of a
subtropical climate.

Legend, however, has a different explanation for Guilin's
topography. There was once a time, the story goes, when the South Sea
was threatening to overflow into Guangxi Province and drown many
thousands of people. But an Immortal took pity on the people of
Guangxi and devised a scheme to save them. He decided to move all
the hills in the north of the province to the south in order to block all
possible inroads of the sea. So he turned the northern hills into
thousands of black goats, and let the flocks stray southwards. As the
goats swarmed over the area round Guilin, a strange gust of wind swept
across the plain, and the goats immediately became hills again — in the
position where they now stand.

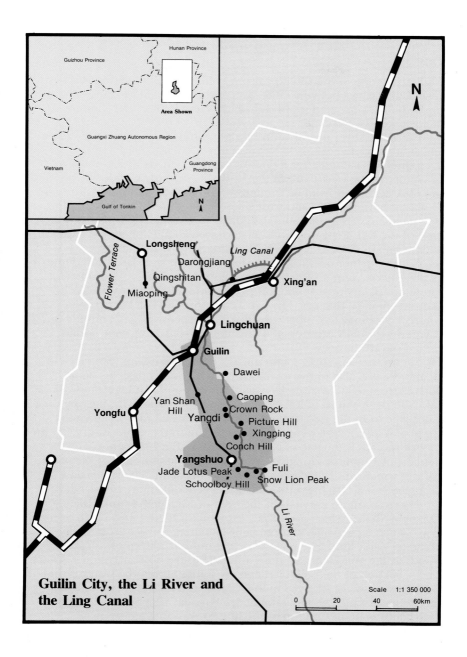

**Guilin City, the Li River and
the Ling Canal**

Scale 1:1 350 000

Sights in and around Guilin

Peaks

A climb up one of the steep peaks in Guilin is well rewarded with spectacular views both en route, and from the top. The climbs are not too arduous, since paths and steps have been built to the summits of the best known hills.

There are several peaks jutting right out of the centre of the town which are easy to get to.

Fubo Hill, named after a famous general, stands in the north part of Guilin on the west bank of the Li River, offering wonderful views of the river and town from its summit. Steps leading up the hill are to be found on both the east and west sides, and by the Returned Pearl Cave (see page 33). Tang and Song Buddhist carvings fill this cave at the base of the hill. Half-way up is an enormous bell (weighing 2.5 tons) and an outsized cooking pot, both formerly used in a temple.

A little further north is **Diecaishan**, which is translated sometimes as the Hill of Many Colours, and sometimes as Folded Brocade Hill. There are plenty of stopping-off points along the way if you do not want to climb to the top. The path leads through the Wind Cave, where a cool breeze supposedly blows in all seasons. Its walls are covered with inscriptions and with some 90 statues of the Buddha carved out of the rock.

For an exciting sheer climb up 306 steps, **Duxiufeng** (Solitary Beauty Peak), also in the town centre, is a good choice. Its name derives from a line written by a poet of the Southern Dynasties who said 'the peak shines in full glory by itself, high above the surrounding landscape.' On the east of the hill is a cavern said to have been the study of Yan Yanzhi, a magistrate of Guilin in the fifth century. At the foot of the hill is the site of a palace, built in the 14th century by the nephew of Emperor Hongwu. Remnants of the entrance of the old palace, which was called Wangcheng, still remain. The site is now occupied by the Guangxi Provincial Teachers Training College.

There are more carvings at the base of **Elephant Trunk Hill** (Xiangbi Shan), which is on the west bank of the Li, just south of the city. This is a particularly prominent landmark viewed from the boat going to Yangshuo. The huge rock, resembling a drinking elephant, stands at the confluence of the Taohua (Peach Blossom) and Li Rivers. The reflection of the arch of Elephant Trunk Hill in the water is said to be the exact image of a full moon. Hence the arch is called Moon in the Water Arch. The Samantabhadra Pagoda, which dates from the 16th century, stands on top of the hill.

A legendary account of the origins of the rock tells of an elephant, which became ill in Guilin and was left to die there by the Heavenly Emperor whose army was sweeping across south China. But a kind old man rescued the elephant and nursed it back to health. This made the emperor angry, and he returned to Guilin with some soldiers to punish the elephant. After fighting off the soldiers for several days, the exhausted elephant was caught unawares, just as it was taking a drink in the river, and stabbed to death from behind. But its body became rock and has remained standing by the river ever since.

On the east side of the river, across Jiefang Bridge, is **Seven Star Hill** (Qixing Shan), so called because of its seven peaks arranged as the stars of the Big Dipper (Ursa Major).

The hill is in **Seven Star Park** which includes the beautiful **Flower Bridge** (Huaqiao), a covered, arched structure which was built in 1540. Standing on the bridge, an anonymous writer of the 18th century wrote:

> After the rain the air is so clear one can see the wild colours far away.
> On the paddy fields the corn leaves are a deep green,
> Reaching to the slender waists of the farm girls
> All this I gather standing on the Flower Bridge on a fine day.

Also located in the park is the instantly recognizable **Camel Hill** (Luotuo Shan). Two rivers flow through the park — the Li and the Xidong — which also contains Seven Star Cave (see below), a zoo and a children's playground.

Caves

The scenery of Guilin is as extraordinary below ground as it is above. Prehistoric rivers running through the ancient limestone have carved giant caverns and fantastic grottos where the slow drip of lime-rich water has, over the millennia, created an amazing collection of stalactites and stalagmites.

Reed Flute Cave (Ludiyan), a 15-minute ride north from the Li River Hotel, is the most celebrated of the caverns. At one time the entrance was disguised by a clump of reeds used by the locals to fashion musical instruments, hence its name. Inside is a multi-coloured 'Disneyland' of fantasy, which is either tasteless or pure magic depending on your viewpoint.

Seven Star Cave (Qixingyan) is on the east side of the river in Seven Star Park. The first chamber is exceptionally large and is decorated with the slogan 'The Chinese Communist Party is the core of the leadership of all the Chinese People' carved in characters the height of a man, high on its wall. On a hot summer's day the thousand-

metre walk through the cool cave is a welcome respite from the more
strenuous activity above ground.

Returned Pearl Cave (Huanzhudong) is below Fubo Hill. Visitors
usually combine a visit to the cave with the climb up the hill,
recuperating on the way down at a small teahouse with an attractive
view across the river towards Seven Star Hill. Below, locals do their
laundry in the shallows and fishermen squat motionless on their fragile
bamboo rafts. Legend tells of another fisherman who long ago stole
the pearl belonging to the dragon which lived in the cave. Later,
overcome by remorse, the fisherman returned the pearl and
presumably he fished happily ever after. Here also is the Thousand
Buddha Cliff with its 300 carvings dating from the Tang and Song
periods. Locals sell paintings and rubbings of calligraphy taken from
the walls of the cave.

Li River Boat Trip

'The river forms a green gauze belt, the mountains are like blue jade
hairpins,' wrote the celebrated ninth-century poet, Han Yu. For many
travellers in China the high point of their entire trip has been the
breathtaking outing along the Li River. This is the finest way to see the
full panorama of the 'mountain and water' scenery of Guilin.

The river rises and falls with the seasons and is at its highest
between May and September when it is possible to cruise the entire 83
kilometres (52 miles) from Guilin to Yangshuo. When the river is low,
airconditioned buses take tourists to Yangdi Village, a little over an
hour's ride from Guilin. Snaking between the peaks, the road abruptly
sweeps down into the fertile Li River valley. On the banks, flat-
bottomed river boats wait for passengers. The boats are pulled down
the river past rocky crags, villages and bamboo groves, over shallows
and rapids, passing the fishermen with their cormorants and local
people selling fruit from small sampans. A simple lunch is cooked on
board during the trip. The number of boats doing this trip increases
annually. Up to 50 a day set off for Yangshuo during peak months in
1987, so it is hardly surprising that the small town of Yangshuo is
overrun with tourists every afternoon. Tickets for the boat trip are
expensive (Rmb50), but this includes the bus-ride back to Guilin. They
may be bought at a number of outlets, including CITS. The boat piers
are along Binjiang Lu in the centre of town.

The Li River tourist boats used to take passengers from Yangshuo
back up the river to Guilin for a fraction of the cost of the downstream
trip. But this practice has been largely discontinued because the boats
became overcrowded.

Yangshuo

'The scenery of Guilin is the finest in the world, the scenery of Yangshuo is the best in Guilin.' So goes the old saying, and indeed the small riverside town of Yangshuo still retains much of its attraction. But its charms have not gone undiscovered; every afternoon, tourists from the Li River boats spill onto Yangshuo's tiny quay, and roam through the town before returning to Guilin by coach.

Yangshuo itself can accommodate up to 200 visitors a night in modest lodgings, and the town has become a key stop on any backpacker's China tour. As a result, even though the town cannot claim to offer many insights into rural Chinese life, it has become a pleasant and easy place to visit. If you are travelling to Yangshuo from Wuzhou, you will probably find people to put you on the right bus in Wuzhou and give you the business cards of Yangshuo hotels. Once in Yangshuo, it is easy to find English speakers at the hotels and in the many small restaurants that have sprung up to cater to the tourists. When you want to leave the town the hotel will book your bus ticket for you (or even a train leaving from Guilin). Buses leave for Guilin throughout the day, and there are also buses to Liuzhou, Wuzhou and Xingping.

Recommended hotels are the **Junfeng Inn** (Rmb6 for a single room), the **Zhuyang Hotel** (Rmb10 for a double room with a private bath), the older **Xilangshan Hotel** (double rooms are Rmb10) and the **Yangshuo Hotel**, which is the most upmarket (a double room with private toilet and shower is Rmb44). CITS is located in the Yangshuo Hotel.

Bicycles can be hired, and any of the dirt trails that branch off the main road into the hills are worth exploring.

All hotels in town offer boat tours on the river. Some are night tours when local fishermen will take visitors out cormorant fishing. A pleasant afternoon trip is to take a bicycle on the 45-minute ferry ride to Fuli, and then cycle back to Yangshuo. A longer boat trip is to the beautiful riverside town of Xingping, set in scenery which some claim is even more dramatic than around Yangshuo. The boat trip takes three hours, and you should return the same day since there is no hotel in Xingping. It is also possible to go to Xingping on the local buses which leave throughout the morning.

The hill in Yangshuo Park is worth climbing for its dramatic view from the summit of the town and nearby karst formations. For a swim, go to the quay, and head down the riverbank for a few minutes to a swimming spot which attracts many travellers.

Not far from Yangshuo is a splendid medieval banyan tree, which provides a pleasant stop-off point en route back to Guilin. Visitors can sit in the shade of the tree with soft drinks, or walk across a causeway into the village that lies amidst the paddy fields. From there it is a 90-minute drive to Guilin.

Ming Tombs

To the northeast of Guilin, at the foot of Yaoshan, is the site of the tombs of 11 Ming-Dynasty (1368–1644) kings of the region. All the superstructure was destroyed during the Qing Dynasty (1644–1911), and some tombs were sacked, but one has recently been reconstructed. Several of the statues along the Spirit Way are there. A hall has been turned into a small museum, showing the whole tomb complex, the construction process and exhibiting some artifacts from the tombs. Unfortunately, none of the explanations are in English. Although this in no way compares with the tombs in Beijing or Nanjing, the setting in Guilin's magnificent countryside makes a visit worthwhile. A few hundred metres to the west of the tomb, surrounded by pines, are some Ming-Dynasty stone carvings of animals and guardians. This is a favourite picnic spot. The site is about 6 kilometres (4 miles) out of town, and can be reached by taxi or by bicycle.

Xing'an and the Ling Canal

Xing'an is a market town with some 280,000 inhabitants 60 kilometres (45 miles) north of Guilin on the railway line or a two-hour journey by road. It is often included in sightseeing programmes for visitors and, although remarkably picturesque in itself, the real attraction is the ancient Ling Canal.

In the third century BC, the first ruler of a unified empire in China, the Emperor Qin Shihuangdi, ordered the digging of a canal to link two rivers, the Xiangjiang (which flows into the Yangzi) and the Tanshui (which flows into the Pearl River), so joining the great water systems of central and southern China. A huge block of masonry was positioned to divide the Xiangjiang, and divert some of its water into the Ling Canal.

The canal has been modified and improved a number of times since then. It was extensively renovated in 1979. Sections of the canal and some of the 36 former locks can still be seen. Visitors are able to enjoy a peaceful walk along its banks starting from the town of Xing'an, passing the spot where three of the emperor's generals, who supervised the construction of the canal, are supposed to be buried. Further on is a large rock called the Feilaishi (The Rock Which Flew There) and the Temple of the Four Sages (Sixianci) which faces the canal. The walk ends where the waters of the Xiangjiang are diverted into the canal.

Canton

Getting to Canton

By Air China's national carrier CAAC (Civil Aviation Administration of China) flies from Hong Kong to Canton daily. New Hong Kong-based airline Dragonair flies regular charters on Monday, Tuesday, Wednesday, Friday and Sunday (US$40 one way).

It is possible to reach Canton by air from every major city in China on CAAC, and China United Airlines (a new commercial airline launched by the People's Liberation Army) flies to a number of major cities from Foshan airport, just outside Canton. There are also weekly international flights to Canton from Bangkok, Manila and Singapore.

Within Guangdong Province there are air links between Canton and Shantou, Meixian (the airport is at Xingning), Zhanjiang, Haikou and Sanya.

By Rail The most common way to reach Canton is by train from Hong Kong. There are four express trains daily that leave from Hung Hom (Kowloon) Station and take approximately three and a half hours (US$27 one way). The line is being upgraded, and while the work is underway there may be delays in the service. There are two departures early morning, and two in the middle of the day. From Canton to Hong Kong there are morning and late afternoon departures. Passengers from Hong Kong go through customs and immigration formalities upon arrival at Canton Station.

Trains between Canton and Beijing take three days and two nights. From Canton to Shanghai is a 35-hour trip. Canton to Guilin is 17 hours and the through trip to Kunming from Canton is 41 hours.

Via Shenzhen A cheaper but longer train trip to Canton involves going to the Hong Kong-China border at Shenzhen, where passengers go through immigration, and then buying a ticket for a local Canton-bound train. Although painfully slow immigration formalities in Shenzhen have greatly speeded up in recent months (except on Hong Kong's public holidays when many thousands of Hong Kong Chinese visit Guangdong), the whole trip to Canton takes around five hours.

Another possibility is to travel to Canton from the border by taxi. In Shenzhen, Canton-bound taxis wait near the railway station touting for custom. The asking price in 1987 was around US$50−100. If you are taking a taxi from Canton to Shenzhen, find out in advance what time the border with Hong Kong closes — immigration officials do not adhere rigidly to a timetable. For budget travellers there are bus services from Shenzhen to Canton.

By Boat In the past five years boat services from Hong Kong to Canton and other ports of Guangdong Province have proliferated.

Perhaps the nicest, and certinly the most romantic way to reach Canton is by overnight passenger liner. Each evening at 9 pm a ship leaves Hong Kong, passes up the Peal River, and reaches Canton ten hours later. There are two Chinese-run ships, the *Xinghu* and *Tianhu* that depart (and return) on alternate nights. The *Xinghu* is larger and has five classes. Super-deluxe gives a suite with brass fixtures, wooden cupboards and private bathroom, while the cheapest ticket buys a reclining seat for the night.

There are several hydrofoils during the day between Hong Kong and Canton that take only three hours. They leave Hong Kong in the early morning and return early afternoon (US$19 one way).

Boat departures are from Tai Kok Tsui in Kowloon. Allow plenty of time when leaving from or arriving at this pier because all services and facilities, from baggage handling to immigration, are severely over-taxed. Enquiries about ticketing and boat schedules can be made to Chu Kong Shipping, Hong Kong (tel. 5-408792; tlx. 71795) or to a number of Hong Kong travel agents.

Getting around Canton

With its geometric street plan and recognizable landmarks, Canton offers fine opportunities for independent exploration. But traffic jams have recently become a regular feature of Canton life, and the large number of roadworks throughout the city aggravate the situation. Particularly disruptive is the construction of a flyover the length of Renmin Lu, but this is due to be finished in 1988.

Canton has one of the largest taxi fleets in China and, unlike in some Chinese cities, they do cruise the streets. At hotels, the railway station and major public buildings, you can usually step straight into a taxi. On the streets you would rarely have to wait more than a couple of minutes before hailing one.

Canton's taxis have meters that are reliable: discrepancies in the fares exist because many types of cars are used as taxis. The fancy ones (Toyota, Citroen, Nissan) cost more per kilometre than the more battered vehicles. Although tipping is not officially permitted, it has become an accepted practice. Flagfall ranges from Rmb1.80–2.40. After midnight taxi-drivers add a 13% surcharge. The six-kilometre (4-mile) journey from the airport to the Trade Fair Exhibition Hall costs round Rmb6, although taxis may try to turn off the meter and charge you more.

Public transport is good, though the numerous buses and trolley-buses that crisscross the city are invariably crowded. Bus fares, which amount to a few *fen* only, are paid to a conductor upon boarding.

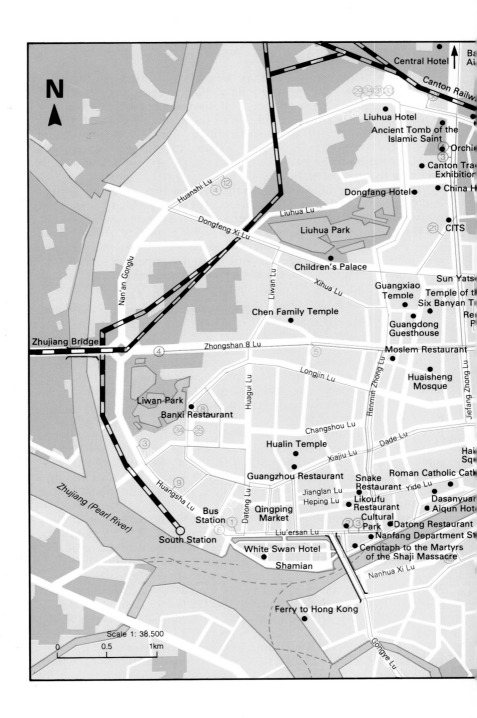

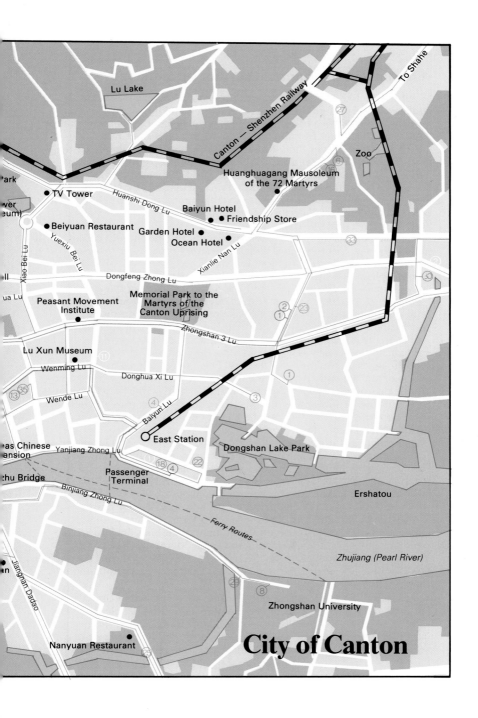

City of Canton

Canton and the Cantonese — an Introduction

Canton is unlike any other Chinese city. And its people — over three million in and around the city, with another 50 million in the surrounding province of Guangdong — have a character of their own, in many ways different from the people in other regions of China.

With a tradition of thinking for themselves, of not accepting easily the dictates of rulers far away to the north, the people of Canton have always had closer links with the outside world than most other Chinese people. Today, the Cantonese still retain a distinctive quality — they have their own cuisine, their own excitable approach to living, and their own racy, idiomatic dialect which is quite incomprehensible to Chinese speakers from other regions.

If China were compared to Europe, the Cantonese would be the Mediterranean people, the Sicilians or Southern Italians. Northern Chinese tend to find the Cantonese a noisy, passionate people. Some have explained away the Cantonese temperament by relating it to the city's climate, which is hot, humid and damp for much of the year.

Canton lies just within the tropics, and the climate doubtlessly contributes much to the city's special atmosphere — a contrasting landscape of greenery, parks and trees, mingling with old temples, sprawling factories, crowded backstreets, and new public buildings in the wide main boulevards. The greenness of the lush subtropical countryside comes right into the centre of the city. From the hundreds of square miles of alluvial delta to the south of Canton, rich supplies of vegetables, fruits, pigs and poultry fill the city's markets, and, well within city limits, the visitor will come across unexpected fields of rice or fruit gardens.

The fertile surrounding countryside of Guangdong Province has always been famous for its fruit, especially lychee. These have rough skins and a hard stone, but the pale juicy flesh is delicious. During the lychee season in mid summer, the people bring in the fruit from the countryside on handcarts and bicycles to sell in the city streets. It is said that, in the past, the Emperor would send post-haste from Beijing to get the best of the lychee crop for a favourite mistress.

The Cantonese are a people who love flowers. The city's first flower fairs were held in the 18th century, when fragrant flowers were used in the processing of tea. Today, in the autumn, thousands flock to see the spectacular chrysanthemum exhibition in the Memorial Park to the Martyrs of the Canton Uprising. At Chinese New Year, during Canton's short winter, the parks are full of displays of dahlias, chrysanthemums and peach blossoms.

Throughout much of the year, because of the climate, Canton's life goes on outside. Whatever the time of day, crowds of people throng the streets — especially the alleyways reached by moongates from the main arteries. There is a restless neighbourbood activity — people visiting or returning from the market, stopping at wayside stalls for fruit or for a cup of that bitter herbal brew that the Cantonese find so health-giving. There are endless groups of children, playing, chasing each other, or absorbed at a small table in the writing of Chinese characters. The warm summer nights are alive with the talk and laughter of Cantonese families and groups of young people, taking the air, strolling to the public parks where special concerts and displays are given for very low prices.

Canton is a city famous for rebellion. In earlier times it was a remote area to which insubordinate princes and ministers were exiled. Over a thousand miles from China's capital city, Beijing, Canton's people have often ignored imperial edicts. As the facade of the last of the Qing Emperors began to crumble in the second half of the 19th century, it was in Canton that the great Chinese revolutionary, Sun Yatsen, worked for the final downfall of the Qing Dynasty in 1911, bringing to an end more than 2,000 years of imperial rule.

Dr Sun Yatsen, founder of the Guomindang — the Nationalist party — and revered by all his countrymen as the founder of modern China, was born near Canton, and holds a special place in the hearts of the Cantonese people. A fine Memorial Hall to Sun Yatsen, built in 1925 after his death, is one of the sights most proudly shown to foreign visitors to Canton.

Another reminder of Canton's contribution to China's revolution is the Peasant Movement Institute, which celebrates the period that Mao Zedong spent in Canton. In 1925 and 1926, Mao, together with some other communists including Zhou Enlai, taught revolutionary ideas to cadres and peasants at the Peasant Movement Institute, looking ahead to the time when the Communist Party would break away from the Nationalists and take over China.

Canton has been a great trading port for hundreds of years. More outward-looking than most of the Chinese, the Cantonese have always been keenly aware of foreign thinking and techniques. Long before Shanghai became established as China's greatest international business and banking centre, the merchants of Canton were doing big business with distant countries. The Pearl River was full of foreign ships and many traders from abroad came to settle in the city. As far back as the eighth century, during the Tang Dynasty, more than a hundred thousand foreign traders and their families — mostly Arabs, the great international merchants of those days — lived in Canton. In the 16th century came the Portuguese, followed by other European traders.

As China's only government-sanctioned foreign trading port, Canton inevitably became the focus of the British attempt to impose free trade on China in the 19th century. With the Chinese defeat in the Opium Wars of the 1840s, Western influence in Canton increased even more, and Shamian Island was set up as a British and French concession area within the city. With its imposing Victorian buildings and European-style churches, this small island in the Pearl River is still a vivid reminder of the earlier powerful foreign presence in Canton.

Canton, the home of the Chinese Export Commodities Fair, remains today at the forefront of China's foreign trade. Now that the Government plans to bring China abreast of the most advanced countries of the world by the end of the 20th century, Canton, as one of 14 coastal cities selected for special economic development, must play a crucial role. Exports flowing out through Canton will help pay for the modern technology that China so urgently needs. Big modernization schemes are under way, and Huangpu, the city's port 36 kilometres (15 miles) south of Canton, is being turned into a modern container port.

Of the large numbers of Chinese that have left their country to look for work abroad, it is the Cantonese who make up the greatest proportion. Hundreds of thousands of Cantonese men went down to Southeast Asia to work for the tin mining or plantation companies of Malaya, Vietnam and Indonesia, or on the timber estates of Borneo. There is not a country in the Far East without its hard-working Chinese minority group. Some have prospered as big traders and bankers, some have stayed on the land as farmers, and many of Southeast Asia's shops are run by the Cantonese. So dominant is the Cantonese influence throughout the Far East, that the Cantonese dialect often serves as a lingua franca amongst the Chinese traders.

Other emigrants have, of course, found their way to Europe and the United States. And the Cantonese outflow continues today, sometimes legally with exit permits, sometimes illegally, by avoiding police and army patrols, and crossing by land or sea into Hong Kong.

Like the other great cities of China, Canton has witnessed much change this century. Well within living memory, Canton was notorious for luxury and official corruption which existed side by side with abject poverty and hunger. Many thousands of people lived and worked in boats on the Pearl River and the overcrowded canals. At night, says one former visitor, the river 'reeked of perfume and opium'. Now all is changed. The canals are filled up, and the municipal apartments to which most of the river-dwellers have been moved are pointed out to visitors. Contronted with the thousands of bicycles on the streets, and the general prosperity, a visitor to Canton is easily persuaded that the great gulf between the rich and poor has now gone.

The Cantonese are capable of absorbing change rapidly, without difficulty. In the last five years, changes in the outward appearance of the city have accelerated dramatically. These are signs of ever-increasing new business and industry — more building, more cars on the roads, and large billboards displaying commercial advertisements in the streets. Restrictions on dress have all but disappeared. And, because Canton lies so close to Hong Kong and the outside capitalist world, the Cantonese have found it easier to acquire jeans, hi-fi equipment, and colour television sets than the people in other Chinese cities. The large numbers of visiting relatives from Hong Kong are always expected to arrive in Canton laden down with presents.

The new generation of Cantonese

Yet, in spite of the changes, the essential character of the Cantonese people remains intact. The first-time visitor to Canton will soon realize that the Cantonese reputation for ingenious craftsmanship is still justified, that their keen business sense and interest in money is as strong as ever, and their love of good food and their garrulous nature still survive.

Maps in English and Chinese showing bus routes are available at
hotels, kiosks and bookshops (see map on page 42). Two useful routes
are number 7 which runs from the China Hotel to Beijing Lu, and
number 6 which crosses the city from the Garden Hotel in the
northeast down to Shamian Island.

Small three-wheeled vehicles provide an informal taxi service,
although their fares nearly equal those of taxis. They have no meters
and prices should be settled before heading off. A trip across town,
from the Pearl River to the main station, is about Rmb8.

There are many public ferries that cross the Pearl River and travel
to small piers beyond the city centre. These offer an exciting way to
see the port of Canton and its water life.

Walking is the best way to see Canton — except in summer when it
can be unbearably hot and humid. Even if your time is limited, plan to
spend some of it on the busy streets, exploring the shops, wandering in
the parks or strolling along the river. Many sights are within walking
distance of the cluster of hotels in Canton's northern districts. Shamian
Island and the nearby Qingping market are other interesting places to
wander.

Bicycles are for hire 8 am—7 pm in a small shop on Shamian Island
opposite the lower level entrance to the White Swan Hotel. The cost
per hour is 90 *fen*. Canton's congested roads make cycling a less
attractive proposition than in many other Chinese cities.

Hotels in Canton

Business visitors and tourists to Canton have a wide range of hotels to
select from. At the top end of the market are three excellent
international-class hotels: the China, the Garden and the White Swan.
As a spin-off from these new international-class hotels, service and
facilities at the medium-range Chinese-run hotels have improved
markedly over the past few years.

In Canton's standard hotels guests should expect to find
airconditioning, direct dial facilities, fridges, television, Western and
Chinese restaurants, some English-speaking staff and possibly 24-hour
room service. Most of Canton's hotels have telex facilities, but
confirmed reservations are still not always possible. Maintenance and
service in the city's standard hotels is on the whole better than in
equivalent hotels in other cities in China.

For much of the year finding a room in Canton is no problem. But
for the few weeks during the Canton Trade Fair (mid April—mid May
and mid October—mid November) it can be a battle to get a decent
room. Rates during those hectic weeks can be as much as double the

usual figure, and stringent no-show rules are applied (usually an advance deposit is required). At other times of the year, it is always worth investigating discounts; a low season discount (December—early March and mid summer) can be as much as 50%.

Deluxe

China Hotel (Zhongguo Dajiudian)
Liuhua Lu
tel. 666888
tlx. 44888
fax. 86-20-677014

中国大酒店
流花路

Double rooms US$68—90; suites US$130—175; all major credit cards accepted

This US$125-million complex, opened in 1983 and run by Hong Kong-based management company New World Hotels International, is more of a mini-city than a mere hotel. It comprises residential expatriate apartments, a carpark, shops which range from florist and delicatessen to a large Friendship Store, together with a fully-equipped multi-purpose function room seating up to 1,200, a business centre, ticketing office, outdoor pool, bowling alley, health centre, and a large selection of restaurants with menus ranging from pseudo street-stall food to high-class European.

The China scores on location for businessmen, being opposite the Trade Fair Exhibition Hall, and just three minutes from the old railway station (although when the planned new railway station is completed on the other side of town, trains from Hong Kong will arrive there instead). Next door, in the Dongfang, several useful foreign trade offices have representatives.

Garden Hotel (Huayuan Jiudian)
368 Huanshi Dong Lu
tel. 338989
tlx. 44788

花园酒店
环市东路

Double rooms US$60—95; executive floor US$85, 95; suites US$135—200; all major credit cards accepted

This is another vast complex, opened in 1984, with over 1000 rooms and similar facilities to the China Hotel. Run by the Hong Kong-based Peninsula Group, the Garden has a residential block, offices, restaurants that range from local Cantonese to elegant European, a disco, a health club and squash courts, swimming pool, business centre, large shopping arcade (especially good for souvenirs) and flexible convention centre which can take 1,800 at a sitting. There is a Friendship Store opposite. The executive floor is recommended for its helpful service and rapid check-in and check-out service. A few self-catering rooms and apartments are also available in the hotel for longer-staying guests. Transport to the Garden, a headache in the past, has eased with the construction of a flyover which has cut down the time to the Trade Fair Exhibition Hall, or the railway station, to around ten minutes.

White Swan Hotel (Baitiane Binguan)
Shamian Island
tel. 886968
tlx. 44688
fax. 861188

白天鹅宾馆
沙面

Double rooms Rmb333, 407 (with view); suites from Rmb518; all major credit cards accepted

Compared with the China and Garden Hotels, the 1,000-room White Swan offers a more tranquil environment, with a superb location on the old foreign enclave of Shamian Island. Best views over the Pearl River are to be had from the eighth floor upwards. A member of 'Leading Hotels of the World', the White Swan is run by arguably the most successful local Chinese management team in China. Hong Kong-Chinese partners have helped keep the hotel up to international standards since its opening in 1982. Recent additions include an attractive riverside garden, a second swimming pool, a competitively-priced health club offering all the facilities one would expect from an international hotel. A new business centre is under construction, and the completion of a flyover along Renmin Lu, the main thoroughfare to the Trade Fair Exhibition Centre area, will improve transportation which to date has been a deterrant for business visitors. The White Swan has always been a favourite with foreign tourists. Its leafy atrium, with waterfalls, rocks and bridges is famous through China, and Chinese tourists still come to admire the decor and photograph each other there. Food matches the other two top hotels, with a European grillroom, a Japanese restaurant, as well as good Cantonese and northern Chinese restaurants.

First-class

**Central Hotel
(Zhongyang Jiudian)**
Guoji Lu
tel. 678331
tlx. 44664

中央酒店
国际路

Double rooms Rmb170, 210; suites Rmb290, 360, 900

Attached to the newly built exhibition hall which belongs to Guangdong International Trade and Exhibition Corporation, this 234-room hotel is located a little out of town on the airport road. It is only ten minutes from the China Hotel and Trade Fair Exhibition Hall, and taxis are readily available. Rooms are pleasant, although standard ones are on the small side. The Central is run by a small Hong Kong management company who have brought in some 30 Hong Kong Chinese to head up the local staff. The Guangdong International Trade and Exhibition Corporation runs the adjoining, vast exhibition hall and an office block (which largely houses its own offices). The Central has an outdoor swimming pool, a coffee shop, Chinese restaurant and business centre.

Dongfang Hotel
Liuhua Lu
tel. 669900
tlx. 44439

东方宾馆
流花路

Double rooms Rmb220; suites from Rmb280

Until the China, Garden and White Swan opened, the 1,200-room Dongfang was the best Canton had to offer. It consists of an old Russian-style eight-storey wing which dates back to 1961 together with a newer shoddily constructed 11-storey wing. The proximity to the Trade Fair Exhibition Hall continues to be a major advantage for business visitors. The hotel contains a Foreign Trade Arcade which houses 11 foreign-trade related offices, including divisions on law, taxation, investment, and the Guangzhou Foreign

People's Bridge, from
Shamian Island

Trade Corporation. Chinese management at the Dongfang has fought hard to keep up with facilities offered at the major new hotels. It has its own entertainment centre (with tennis courts, bowling alley pool, health club) shopping arcade, food street, disco, xerox counter, telegraph service, and beauty salon. A warren of restaurants is to be found on the ground floor, while the eighth floor has 22 banqueting rooms. Some of the Dongfang's improvements have been of dubious merit — two scenic elevators which jerk up the Russian facade, an abundance of electronic games, and an overhead walkway held up by knarled cement tree trunks. But for those who knew the Dongfang in the 70s, the transformation in service and facilities is both dramatic and welcome.

Novotel Jiangnan Hotel
348 Jiangnan Dadao Zhong
tel. 429645

江南大酒店
江南大道中345号

This new 460-room hotel, on the south bank of the Pearl River, was due to open early in 1988. Managed by the French group Novotel, it intends to be a medium-range hotel, with prices about 25% less than those at the Garden, China or White Swan. It is located about 30 minutes' drive from the airport, and close by the pier for Hong Kong-bound ferries. It has a French brasserie, two Chinese restaurants, swimming pool, games room, and health centre.

Standard

Aiqun Hotel
111−3 Yanjiang Yi
Lu
tel. 661445

爱群大厦
沿江一路111-3号

Double rooms Rmb110, 125; suites Rmb160

This 370-room hotel, overlooking the Pearl
River, is made up of two adjoining buildings,
one built in 1937 and the other which was
added in 1966. It was formerly called the
Renmin, or People's, Hotel. The old rooms
have been done up, and airconditioning,
phone, and television added. Its two large
restaurants can accommodate 1,200 diners.

Baiyun Hotel
Huangshi Dong Lu
tel. 333998
tlx. 44698

白云宾馆
环市东路

Double rooms Rmb100

Situated in the northeast of the city, next door
to the Friendship Store and opposite the giant
Garden Hotel, the 720-room Baiyun (White
Cloud) Hotel, notorious in the past for its
poor standards, has recently remodelled itself.
It has a new lobby, coffee shop, disco, new
elevators (a ten-minute wait for elevators used
to be the norm), and a top floor restaurant
and function rooms, affording a magnificent
view of the city and the White Cloud
Mountain. Rooms have also been improved,
although service still falls well below
international standards.

**Guangdong
Guesthouse**
603 Jiefang Bei Lu
tel. 332950
tlx. 44232

广东迎宾馆
解放北路603号

Double rooms Rmb105−20; suites Rmb230

This 320-room hotel is centrally located off
Renmin Lu, and opposite the Buddhist
Temple of the Six Banyan Trees. It consists of
four blocks — one recently constructed, and
the others renovated — set in a garden. There
is a Western restaurant, coffee shop, Chinese
restaurant, ticket counter and telex service.
This is a favourite with Hong Kong Chinese
businessmen.

**Guangzhou
Guesthouse**
Haizhu Guangchang
tel. 338168

Double rooms Rmb80, 85

This 27-storey grey structure with over 500
rooms was built in 1968 and revamped in
1983. Located in the noisiest part of town,

广州宾馆
海珠广场

overlooking the Pearl River, its higher rooms offer excellent views. The top-floor rooms have been given superior treatment, and rates are higher. There are restaurants on the third floor (where there is dancing in the evening) and 25th floor. At the fifth-floor 'music tea house' Chinese and foreign music is performed in the evenings.

Liuhua Guesthouse
Renmin Bei Lu
tel. 668800, 678398
tlx. 44298

流花宾馆
人民北路

Double rooms Rmb120

This 660-room hotel is conveniently situated near the railway station. It consists of two buildings; best rooms are in the new wing which is also slightly less noisy. There is a coffee shop and eight restaurants, most serving Cantonese food; food from Chaozhou and Dongjiang is also available.

Nanhu Guesthouse
Nanhu Gongyuan
tel. 776367
tlx. 44511

南湖宾馆
南湖公园

Double rooms Rmb70

The Nanhu Guesthouse is a lakeside resort, some 16 kilometres (10 miles) northeast of Canton in attractive countryside, largely catering to Hong Kong and overseas Chinese, and to local holiday-makers. The Chinese-managed hotel consists of two low-rise blocks, each with 150 rooms, reminiscent of a US motel. Six restaurants serve Cantonese and Western meals and there are souvenir shops, bars and a discotheque. As well as an amusement park, there is a large open-air swimming pool, a shooting gallery, a horse-riding ring, tennis courts, a dodgem car arena and a pond for bump-boats. On the lake there are paddle boats, plus fishing facilities.

Ocean Guesthouse
Huanshi Dong Lu
tel. 765988
tlx. 44638
cable 6054

远洋宾馆
环市东路

Double rooms Rmb140, 160

Opened in 1987, the Ocean shares the tower block with the offices of China's shipping giant, COSCO, which owns the hotel. It is five minutes' walk from the Garden Hotel, in the fast developing northeast of the city. Facilities are similar to those in most of Canton's new hotels, but unique is the lobby which features porthole-shaped fish tanks. There are secretarial services, a ticketing service, Chinese and Western restaurants, a snooker hall and disco, popular with Canton's young *nouveau-riche*.

Overseas Chinese Mansion (Huaqiao Dasha)
2 Qiaoguang Lu
tel. 336888
cable 3307

华侨大厦
侨光路 2 号

Double rooms Rmb130

Originally built in 1957 as a 'home' for visiting Chinese, the hotel will now accept individual foreign travellers. It is virtually always full and seething with people of all ages who congregate in the noisy lobby. Management here are specially proud of the hotel's food — a vital aspect of a visit for any Chinese. There are two Cantonese restaurants and a good Chaozhou restaurant. Not all the 770 rooms have airconditioning.

Budget

Guangzhou Youth Hostel (Waishibu Zhaodaisuo)
Si Jie, Shamian
tel. 884248, 889251

广州外事部招待所
沙面四街

A meeting place for backpackers, the Guangzhou Youth Hostel is well located on Shamian Island, almost opposite the lower entrance to the White Swan Hotel. A room with toilet is Rmb40; with a shared bath Rmb26, and a dormitory bed is Rmb8–10.

Cantonese Food

China travellers have come to accept a misleading paradox this past decade: Cantonese food is the best in Asia, but the food in Canton is the worst in Asia.

The first proposition is an understatement. Ingredients, techniques, history and imagination have undoubtedly made Canton the region with the finest cuisine in China, Asia and, arguably, the world. The second statement was never totally true, but it is certainly the case that the cuisine of Canton, until recently, never lived up to its elevated reputation. In fact, one had to go to Hong Kong, San Francisco, New York, even Singapore, for Cantonese food superior to that of its home.

Fortunately, this is no longer so. It may take time, effort and language ability or friends to search out the great restaurants, but they are certainly there. With rising standards of living, the result of China's economic reforms, the major markets are now better stocked with meat, a plethora of vegetables and seafood. And the herb market stocks the herbs, spices and medicinal animals — from winter worms to lizards, starfish and eels — which give that extra zest to Cantonese cuisine. The restaurants have changed as well. Ten years ago, Canton's chefs had lost their love: not only were the ingredients poor, but the Cultural Revolution had even reached the kitchens. Cadres, not chefs, had taken over the wok. While menus looked all right on paper, in practice dishes were plain and uninteresting.

All is not ideal today, but improvements are noticeable: more English-language menus, more dishes, better prepared. Awards in annual food competitions are no longer given to those who can prepare more for less, as in the old days, but to those who demonstrate imagination and originality.

Yet there are still certain disadvantages to eating out in Canton's restaurants, and any visitor should be aware of these:

Language Without speaking Mandarin or Cantonese, problems are inevitable. The best way is to go with a Chinese-speaking friend. Second best is to go with a large party for the regulation tour group banquet. These may be served up assembly-line style, but visitors are not any the worse for it. Individual visitors may have many problems, some stemming from simple misunderstanding, others from a different attitude towards service. Patience and humour are the best ways to rectify this.

Private versus public The most significant transformation is the opening of privately managed restaurants, frequently with Hong Kong capital behind them. These probably have more imaginative menus, and a more enthusiastic and friendly staff. The decor may be hideously like the most garish Hong Kong eateries, but this seems to please the Cantonese, who equate kitsch with contemporaneity.

Late nights Restaurants which used to close at 10 pm now stay open to the wee hours. But do not expect to get served much after 8 pm. Late hours are mainly for young people, when they sip beer or tea, order a few pastries, and hear music. Hunger pangs can best be satisfied up to midnight either at the hotels or at the enjoyable outdoor markets.

Prices These are relatively expensive, or at least up to Hong Kong prices. Prices on English-language menus are marginally higher than on Chinese menus, but this is simply accepted and is not considered cheating. A meal for four people could cost around Rmb20 a head, while a banquet would start at Rmb50 a head.

Segregation Some years ago, many restaurants were off-limits to foreign visitors. This is no longer the case, but 'voluntary segregation' is still the rule, and foreigners will be guided to the most luxurious floor of the restaurant, with prices to match. Should one wish to dine with the local Chinese, however, one can certainly do so. The reason for the luxury is simply the thought that this is what visitors are more accustomed to.

Why should any visitor to Canton bother to break through these barriers for a simple lunch or dinner? Simply because Cantonese food, when prepared well, is like the best of anything — worth having for its own sake. This cuisine has been served by geography, economics and innovation to be the best, and it wears its crown proudly.

Geographically, Guangdong Province has been blessed by a 1,600-kilometre (1,000-mile) coastline, by a rich alluvial soil and a fertile river delta. This, combined with a subtropical climate and an abundance of freshwater and ocean fish, means that the province has all the ingredients for the varied dishes.

Economically, Canton was the first province, and always the most predominant, in dealing with the West, notably through Macau. The Jesuits of Macau took many of their Mediterranean crops and planted them in border territory, varying Canton's ingredients even more. And while famine has, until recently, been part of the province's history, this has only made the rural people more self-reliant, less wasteful, more innovative in preparing food which utilizes all edible materials.

Since the Cantonese were the first to migrate overseas — not from the city of Canton but from the western side of the province through Macau — Cantonese restaurants were the first Chinese restaurants known to the West, and this spurred the immigrants to develop new recipes to please Western palates.

Cantonese cooking is known for its marinated and roast meats which can be eaten hot or cold at any time. Stir-frying and blanching are typical cooking methods. Steaming is the usual method of preparing fish. Quick-frying is for vegetables and meats, but even here, a minimum of oils are necessary, so Cantonese food is the least oily of all Chinese cuisine. Add to this only the finest sauces, and only when necessary: black bean, garlic, smooth rich oyster sauce, lemon sauce — all of them come from this province.

With such a variety of cooking, the knowledgeable diner has a choice
of very fine restaurants here. One must order judiciously (varying fried,
steamed, quick-fried dishes, cold and warm, meats, poultry, soup and
rice) or leave a banquet up to the chef himself. In fact, you will probably
find it easier to arrange a banquet (which should be booked in advance)
than a simple meal. For breakfast, try and order a variety of *dianxin*
(*dim sum*), for this is a Canton speciality. These *hors d'oeuvres* come in
a multitude of forms, and you can order them off carts as they are
wheeled past your table.

The night markets are also worth a look. Long after the restaurants
have closed, the Cantonese — enjoying a new-found freedom and
relative prosperity — dine on the streets from stalls equipped with fresh
produce and interesting recipes.

The colour and innovation in Cantonese cuisine may be relatively
new, but they only justify the old Chinese proverb: 'Let there be plenty
of food and clothing, and propriety and righteousness will flourish.'

To accompany the food, most foreigners drink tea, the local beer, or
sweet Chinese-produced soft drinks. Chinese wines are mostly very
sweet, although dry grape wines, both red and white, are increasingly
available in places where foreigners eat. There are some excellent rice
wines, such as Shaoxing, although it is not always available. The highly
potent Chinese spirit Maotai, made from sorghum, is good for any
flagging social occasion and is a great stimulus to speechmaking, but it is
an acquired taste. Although imported alcohol is not usually served in
restaurants, it is possible to buy quite a wide range of imported wines
and spirits in hotel shops, as well as Coca-Cola. All Canton's top hotels
have wide-ranging wines and spirits lists.

Restaurants in Canton

Cantonese

Banxi Restaurant
151 Longjin Xi Lu
tel. 889318

泮溪酒家
龙津西路151号

This is one of Canton's most beautiful restaurants, overlooking an artificial lake. The rooms open off a labyrinth of corridors in old Chinese style, with much lattice woodwork and alcoves. There is a lovely garden, with little bridges, peaked tiled roofs and carp in a large fishpond. So attractive is Banxi, though, that it takes visitors for granted and the foreign diner who does not come with a tour group can get short shrift (and large portions for only small groups). But with careful ordering, one can enjoy a classic meal here. The *dim sum* are superb, and the fried rice is as special as the stewed turtle and chicken in tea leaves.

Beiyuan
246 Xiao Bei Lu
tel. 332466, 332471,
332466

北园酒家
小北路318号

For 15 years the Beiyuan has served the foreign community and tour groups well. The Beiyuan is noted for its appealing architecture of moats and little bridges, old-style ebony cabinets and large banquet rooms each with different colour motifs. It offers a good middle-brow banquet, which has little to frighten even the most terrified tourist. Banqueters may sample the famous Cantonese suckling pig, served in two courses. The first course brings the whole pig to the table, with the barbecued skin cut into strips about an inch wide. These are served with pancakes, green onions and a thick sauce made of fermented dough. Next, the meat (along with some of the skin and a fair amount of fat) is brought back with more scallions and more sauce.

The restaurant has a few specialities for which advance orders should be made: fried shrimps, suckling goose with sweet-sour sauce, sweet and sour fish with pinenut seeds and fried duck web with oyster sauce.

Nanyuan
120 Qianjin Lu
tel. 449979, 449441

南园酒家
前进路120号

Renowned as one of the great restaurants of China, the Nanyuan has more than fine cuisine: it has huge gardens with ponds, gates, great bamboo trees, and bridges spanning moats. Then there are no fewer than 20 different restaurants and banquet halls, each with lovely marble furniture, scrolls along the walls, and displays of the traditional Chinese art of framed marble. The food is expensive but equally impressive — soups with chicken, bamboo and pigeon eggs; two-coloured perch balls; beancurd with crabmeat; and fried fresh milk with shrimp. Original recipes include rockfish and chicken rolls — a delicate kind of spring roll, steamed in coconut milk with chicken and ham. Although a good meal here could be costly, the beautiful surroundings and the chance to try interesting dishes make it worth the financial sacrifice.

Likoufu
86 Shisanhang Lu
tel. 882418

利口福
十三行路86号

For over 40 years, the magnificent Likoufu has been serving classical Daliang cuisine, the style which is the foundation of Cantonese cuisine. (Daliang itself is on the road to Macau.) The Koufu chicken is specially famous, but equally well known are the braised spring chicken, crab cutlet with pig-brain, and a great profusion of seafood. The restaurant can accommodate some 1,400 diners, most of whom are aware of the meaning of the restaurant's name — 'Gourmet Luck' — and revel in the dishes.

Datong
63 Yanjiang Xi Lu
tel. 888988,
887345,885933

大同大酒家
沿江西路63号

This famous Cantonese restaurant boasts five floors all decorated differently, and a roof garden. It has the most famous roast suckling pig, and a delicious roast chicken with a coating of honey, rice wine, Chinese vinegar, salt, cardamom, flower pepper, ginger, licorice, cloves and cinnamon. Other specialities are chicken filled with lotus leaves, and the most delicate fried shrimp in milk.

Dasanyuan
260 Changdi Lu
tel. 883277

大三元酒家
长堤路260号

This is Canton's first large joint-venture restaurant, decorated in characteristic gaudy red, with sliding doors, high ceilings, ornate decorations — the style of many traditional-style restaurants in Hong Kong. A fine chicken which is cooked in a clay pot with tea leaves, herbs and soy is served here. Chicken with beans on a hot plate is also especially good, and sautéed shrimp, Sichuan-style, has the peppery taste of that province. One pays a bit more than in other restaurants of this type, but with the private ownership of Dasanyuan, one also gets more imaginative recipes. *Dim sum* is served from 6 am to 4 pm.

Taotaoju
20 Dishipu
tel.885769, 887501

陶陶居
第十甫20号

You could not miss this gaudy restaurant, distinguished by its rooftop pagoda, its inside corridor with ornate mirrors, four vast floors with stages for musicals, masses of private rooms, and space for up to 1,200 guests. Taotaoju advertises itself as being furnished in 'classical Chinese decor', but nowhere is there classical Chinese simplicity. The restaurant entertains foreign tour groups by the score: they are hustled in and out of the private rooms, seem to eat well on the roast suckling pig, the beancurd, the fine winter-melon soup, the pan-fried beef with oyster sauce, and rice noodles from Shahe. One need not wait for autumn to sample the mooncakes, which are famous here (and rightly so, as they seem lighter than most). The fourth floor, which has a decor somewhere between Hong Kong kitsch and a San Francisco 1890s dance-hall, is unfortunately rather pricey — more so than the plainer lower floors.

Guangzhou
2 Wenchang Nan Lu
tel. 884334, 861985

广州酒家
文昌南路2号

One is bound to meet foreign tour groups enjoying their set banquets here, for the Guangzhou has always made a speciality of entertaining overseas visitors. This is not a shortcoming by any means. The restaurant knows how to please foreign guests, whether

with 'ordinary' dishes like crab paste dumplings, steamed chicken in Maotai or fried perch; or with the more esoteric dishes such as duck webs stuffed into steamed chicken, or braised doves with shrimp paste. The architecture is interesting, with the rooms arranged around a tree-filled courtyard. Large groups are probably treated better than smaller parties, but with enough perseverance (and hopefully, a Chinese-speaking friend) even the notable Cantonese specialities can be happily consumed by small groups.

Yijingyuan
183 Yanjiang Xi Lu
tel. 337804

一景园酒家
沿江西路

You would hardly notice this street-corner restaurant, but its friendly informality is a sign of the interesting things going on inside. Yijingyuan is one of Canton's largest privately-owned restaurants, with a highly imaginative menu. Where else could you get whitebait with sliced beef and sour vegetables? No other restaurant would offer so many fresh mushroom soups. And the food tastes as interesting as it sounds. The whitebait comes in a ring of fried rice noodles, the mushrooms come with oyster sauce, ginger, and green onions. Yijingyuan's English-language menu is good (though the serving staff speak little English). The prices are exceptionally moderate, so rightly Yijingyuan attracts backpackers as well as knowledgeable gourmets. Open 24 hours a day (only snacks after 8.30 pm), it has a class and imagination which make up for its unprepossessing interior.

Snake Restaurant (She Canguan)
41 Jianglan Lu
tel. 883811, 883424, 882517

蛇飡馆
浆栏路

This is one of two wild animal restaurants in the city, and though many Chinese eschew this type of food, snake is widely eaten by the Cantonese, who consider it a warming dish in winter. The snakes are caught wild in the forest and served in 30 different snake recipes. Most popular is dragon-tiger-phoenix soup, made with three kinds of meat — snake, cat and chicken. The snake is cut into cubes, the cat into slivers. The cat can be eliminated, to create dragon-phoenix soup which is also cheaper. No English menu is available, but the waiters speak some English. Other wild game is available, as well as ordinary rice and noodles.

Shahe Restaurant
87 Xianlie Dong Lu
Shahe
tel. 775639, 775449, 777239

沙河饭店
先烈东路87号

This is the ultimate rice noodle restaurant. Visitors from throughout China come to this restaurant in Shahe, a town 15 minutes from Canton, famous for its water and rice. They enjoy the lovely second-floor garden restaurant with its marble tables and stone chairs. The fortunate visitors can watch the whole noodle-making process. According to the 600-year-old recipe, the rice noodles are chopped fine, soaked for 12 hours, laid out on bamboo mats and cut a quarter of a centimetre thick. Over 500 kilos of noodles are consumed each day in 40 different ways. Five flavours (sour, sweet, hot, cool-and-bitter, salty), four different grades, dozens of ingredients (mushrooms, bamboo, beef, chicken, pork), 15 chefs and 30 assistants to make the noodles, and over a century on the same site, all make Shahe a unique restaurant. Parties of eight may order the VIP-room banquets.

Pearl River (Zhujiang Haixian Jiujia)
Pier 39, Yanjiang Lu
tel. 882151, 882118

珠江海鲜酒家
沿江西路39号码头

This new restaurant on the banks of the Pearl River is highly rated both by expatriates and locals alike and offers the best seafood in the city. Its seasonal game is also said to be good.

Dicai (Dicai Bingshi)
17−21 Er Malu
Xihao
tel. 887586

This serves some of the best ice cream in town. You do not need a menu or language ability to come to this coffee house. Just point to the dish you want or point to the woman serving the speciality — ice cream with red

的彩冰室
西濠二马路17-21号

beans and fruit. Dicai is very friendly, always filled with young people, cheap, with good soft drinks, and ice cream flavoured with chocolate, vanilla and coconut (so fresh you can practically taste the slivers of coconut fruit).

Chaozhou (Chiu Chow)

Chaozhou Caiguan
Overseas Chinese
Mansion
2nd floor, 10
Guangda Lu
tel. 335094

潮州菜馆
广大路10号华侨大厦
二楼

This restaurant with a 'First Grade Chef' takes pride in serving the best Chiu Chow food in the city. The problem — and a formidable one — is no English menu and probably no English-language speakers. But, one should make the effort, as Chiu Chow food is very different from ordinary Cantonese. The wild goose roast is juicier, with more soy sauce, and the chicken has a special smoked flavour. The sharks' fin is famous for its thickness. Aside from the goose, one should try the special deep-fried fish with its distinctive grainy texture, the shrimp ball with crab and mushroom, and the shrimp in tomato sauce.

Beijing

Beijing Restaurant
10 Er Malu
Xihao
tel. 887964, 887158

北京饭店
西濠二马路10号

There are probably better Beijing-style restaurants in China, but this one has the advantage of offering a rare chance to see Canton's nightlife at close range while you eat. The Beijing is in the centre of the Night Market, so you can sit at a table on the ground floor, open to the street, and watch people enjoy themselves while you sup on the usual North China fare (noodles, steamed and fried dumplings, hotpot) and Cantonese dishes.

Moslem

Moslem Restaurant (Huimin Fandian)
325 Zhongshan Liu Lu
tel. 888991, 888417

回民饭店
中山六路325号

A bit tatty now, but this restaurant has true *halal* food: you will never be served any lard or other pork dish. You will get a fine hotpot of sliced mutton, fish, veal, sliced chicken, beef, prawns. The barbecue sauce is made with vinegar, mustard, ginger, garlic and some secret herbs and spices. They also have curried beef and sliced chicken soup, with the usual noodles. Although not up to the standards of a Beijing Moslem restaurant, this is the only one in town and is worth a try, especially as the English menu is comprehensive. At night, the young bloods of the town, boys and girls, come in for tea, beer and snacks, and listen to a strange medley of Austrian, Greek and Spanish music over the loud-speakers.

Vegetarian

Caigenxiang
167 Zhongshan Liu Lu
tel. 886835

菜根香素飡馆
中山六路167号

This is the best-known vegetarian restaurant in Canton, and for good reason. The upstairs, with its bamboo cubicles and seats and old-style stained glass windows, is charming; the English menu is comprehensive, and the dishes tasty. Apart from the romantic menu names like 'power of Buddha', they have more easily recognized dishes — a dried beancurd with skin looking like a sausage or a 'roast duck' beancurd. The menu changes specialities every so often, so you have to use your imagination when you come across dishes like 'moon shadow on the milky way' (black and white mushrooms and an egg yolk in soup) or 'eight treasures' (eight different beancurds).

Hotel Restaurants

Dining out in the city can be a daunting experience without knowledge of the language, and Canton's top hotels provide a particularly wide range of restaurants and bars for easier, if less adventurous, eating. The hotel restaurants attract expatriates, local Chinese and visitors alike.

The classiest restaurant in Canton for continental food is the elegant **Connoisseur** in the Garden Hotel (see pages 50−56 for hotel addresses and telephone numbers) which is excellent. Emphasis is on *nouvelle cuisine*, and the wine list is unusually extensive for China. **The Roof**, on the 18th floor of the China Hotel, also has a pleasant continental menu, as well as good bird's-eye views of the city and live classical music in the evening. The White Swan's upmarket Western restaurant is the ground-floor **Silk Road** which also has a loyal following of expatriates.

For more informal dining, there are coffee shops in all the joint-venture hotels offering the usual international fare — the White Swan's is recommended for its superb view across the river. Also in the White Swan is the **Songbird Living Room**, which serves inexpensive Mexican food every day 10 am−11 pm. The Garden has a pizza restaurant with specially imported ovens and chefs. The **Hirata** at the White Swan offers good, but expensive, Japanese food — *shabu shabu* and *sukiyaki* cooked at the table costs Rmb250, and *teppanyaki* is from Rmb70 (open 11 am−2.30 pm, 6 pm−9.30 pm).

Recommended Chinese restaurants in hotels are: the popular **Four Seasons** in the China Hotel (open 7 am−10 am, 11 am−3 pm, 5 pm−10 pm) which serves quality Cantonese food (book early for Sunday *dim sum* and during the Trade Fair); the Garden Hotel's **Peach Blossom**, another Cantonese restaurant; and the **Yu Tang Chen Luan** in the White Swan (open 7 am−2.30 pm and 5.30 pm−9.30 pm) which is good for northern and spicy Sichuan food. The Dongfang's huge ground-floor **Jade Palace** can seat 800, and serves good Cantonese food. Service and decor are less polished than in the joint-venture hotels, but the dishes cost less.

Shopping in Canton

Canton has a large number of stores selling famous local products as well as merchandise from other parts of China. The breadth of selections may not be as great as in Shanghai or Beijing, but most tourists in search of souvenirs will find something suitable. Most hotels have shopping arcades which provide a convenient — if more expensive — opportunity to buy souvenirs.

The crowded shops also offer a chance to observe the recent dramatic rise in Canton's living standards. Shops and street markets are packed with a surprisingly diverse selection of goods, which range from shoddily made clothes, shoes and household goods, to export-jeans, imported watches, electronics and sunglasses.

There is a large **Friendship Store** on Huanshi Dong Lu, across the road from the Garden Hotel (open 9 am—9 pm), which is no longer restricted just to foreign buyers. A second Friendship Store (open 9 am—9 pm) is located within the China Hotel complex, and has a good variety of silk blouses, ties, shirts, cashmere sweaters and hand-painted T-shirts.

Antiques which can be exported must have a red seal on them, though not all items bearing red seals are antiques. The days of discovering Ming vases for a few dollars are long gone and good

Free market 'boutique', Guangta Lu, Canton

antiques are hard to find and expensive. However, excellent reproductions can be bought at very reasonable prices. Popular buys are
pottery and porcelain, stone rubbings, hanging scrolls, and jewellery.
The **Canton (Guangzhou) Antique Shop** is at 146 Wende Bei Lu,
just off Zhongshan Lu. Visitors must keep all sales receipts to show
upon departure from China. Prices are similar to or even higher than
prices in Hong Kong and the selection is smaller. There is a similar
shop at the entrance of Guangxiao Temple (see page 80). Both these
accept the usual credit cards, and arrange for packing, shipping and
insurance.

There are several bookshops along Zhongshan Lu and Beijing Lu.
Xinhua Bookshop, 376 Beijing Lu, is the largest in the city and has an
excellent collection of Chinese books on art, history and literature as
well as dictionaries. Provincial maps and colourful propaganda posters
are popular items. The **Children's Bookstore**, 314 Beijing Lu, is always
jammed with children and their parents buying historical comic books,
text, and new publications. Canton's **Foreign Language Bookstore**, 326
Beijing Lu, stocks books in a number of languages printed by the
Foreign Languages Press, as well as some foreign paperbacks,
guidebooks and news magazines. Art books on many aspects of
China's culture and her treasures are handsomely produced.
Translations of Chinese novels and short stories, both modern and
classical, are most reasonably priced, as are dictionaries and booklets
on a wide range of subjects.

Even if you do not visit Foshan, you can find Foshan's famous
pottery in Canton at Friendship Stores and numerous shops along
Zhongshan Lu.

Cantonese handicrafts to keep an eye out for are coloured
porcelain, ivory carving, intricate papercuts and jade carving. The **Jade
Carving Factory**, 15 Xiajiu Lu, is open to the public and allows visitors
to watch the craftsmen close up. It has a shop on the top floor and a
sales outlet at street level.

China's famous silks are bountiful in Canton and are used in
making shirts, blouses, robes, dresses, ties and scarves.

For those interested in calligraphy and the tools of traditional
Chinese painting, the small **Sanduoxuan Cultural Articles Store**, 322
Beijing Lu, sells ink-stones, ink-sticks, paper, beautiful brushes and
brush holders.

The middle section of Zhongshan Lu is a good street for shoppers
who like to browse. There is a remarkable array of shops and items —
Chinese medicines, clothing, photographic studios with elaborate
painted backdrops, fireworks, grocery shops, bamboo bird cages,
carved pipes, wine jugs, embroidery, and even a noodle factory.

The **Changjiang Musical Instrument Shop**, 6—8 Zhongshan Wu Lu, sells traditional instruments, such as *erhu*, *pipa*, numerous drums and bamboo flutes. It also functions as a costume supply shop. Stage swords, spears, masks, head-dresses and magnificent dragon costumes are stacked throughout the store.

Canton's department stores are convenient places to go shopping because of the concentration of goods in a single, often enormous, building. The **Canton Trade Fair Exhibition Hall Store**, across the street from the China and Dongfang Hotels, is conveniently located.

Nanfang Mansion on the busiest section of the waterfront (Yanjing Xi Lu), is Canton's largest store. On the ground floor you can buy umbrellas, cutlery, cosmetics, artificial flowers; a mezzanine floor stocks jade, silver and the usual range of Chinese arts and crafts. The first floor has clothing for children, men and women, as well as bed and table linen. Upstairs on the second floor are household goods, suitcases and shoes, while the third floor has an astonishingly diverse selection of sports and entertainment equipment, with fruit machines, outboard motors, games such as Chinese checkers, records, cassettes and musical instruments.

Entertainment in Canton

Canton by night is far more vibrant than many of China's more staid cities further north. Even though there is nothing to match Hong Kong's sophistication, Canton's street life continues up to midnight, with small roadside restaurants and street markets doing good business, especially during the warm summer months.

Western-style nightlife revolves round the hotels, which offer the standard range of bars and lobby lounges — some with classical music performances in the evening. A particular favourite of the expatriate community is the **Tavern** in the Garden Hotel, an English pub-style bar complete with darts board. For dancing, there is **Parrots**, also at the Garden (tel. 338989), a slick joint-venture disco run by Julianna's (of London, Hong Kong, Singapore, Penang), which attracts a well-dressed Hong Kong Chinese clientèle. **Checkmate**, in the basement of the China Hotel, is another international-style disco, popular with overseas visitors. At the spacious **River Room** at the White Swan a small Filipino band nightly plays more downbeat music (8 pm—1 am).

For a glimpse of local nightlife there are dozens of discos where Canton's new generation of style-conscious pop fans do their best to keep up with Hong Kong trends. The popularity of discos changes as rapidly in Canton as elsewhere, but trendiest in 1987 was the rowdy

Dongshan Hotel (44 Sanyu Lu, Dongshan tel. 773772), where a
relatively high fee of Rmb18 did not deter crowds of young locals from
entry (8 pm—midnight). The noisy **Jade Palace** in the Dongfang Hotel
(tel. 669900) is a favourite with both locals and Hong Kong Chinese.
Live bands, some from Hong Kong, thump out rock, pop and
traditional music from 9.30 pm-midnight. Well-turned out locals also
favour the **Cutty Sark** restaurant in the Ocean Hotel (tel. 765988)
which turns into a disco every night (9 pm-midnight).

Canton has its share of performances of Chinese opera, dance and
acrobatics, but it is hard to find out what is on. Even if you can read
Chinese, the local newspapers do not consistently advertise
performances, and the English-language China Daily rarely carries
information of that kind. Best is to ask at your hotel on arrival, and
buy tickets as soon as possible — any good show sells out rapidly.

Canton has a reasonable spread of sports facilities, although the
best are in the hotels and priority is given to guests. Pools are for hotel
guests only. The White Swan's new health club is attractively located
overlooking the river, and has gym, sauna, steambath, sunbath, squash
courts, a golf driving range, and tennis courts. There is also a tennis
court at the China (book in advance for the evenings or at weekends),
and several less expensive locally-run courts on Shamian Island. The
Garden Hotel has squash courts.

Snooker is popular in Canton, and most hotels have a snooker hall.
There are several bowling alleys in the city; the best, which has
become a fashionable haunt of Canton's *nouveau-riche*, is at the China
Hotel (open 10 am—12.30 am) and there is a smaller foue-lane one at
the Dongfang next door (9.00 am-midnight).

Business Facilities in Canton

Doing business in China is never easy but in Canton facilities have
improved greatly since the economy opened up nine years ago.

Telecommunications have been revolutionized with the
introduction of IDD to an increasing number of overseas countries
(13 at the latest count), Hong Kong and Macau, and 45 places in
China. Nowadays it can be harder to make a local call in Canton than
an international one.

Most hotels for overseas visitors in Canton have telexes (although
operators are not always available) and some have fax machines. But
fully-fledged business centres are still rare. If you are after genuine
secretarial services, competent translation and decent quality work,
use the business centres at the Garden or the China — and be

prepared to spend more than you would for similar services in Hong Kong. If, however, you just have something simple to do, like photocopying, it is cheaper to use local services — but don't entrust anything big to them. The Chinese-run **Dongfang Hotel**, for example, has a copy service centre (tel. 669900 ext 7858). It is open 8 am—9.30 pm and its charge of Rmb0.30 per sheet is half the cost of the neighbouring China Hotel. It also has a telex room (tel. 69900 ext. 7938; tlx. 44439) which is open 8 am—9 pm.

At the **China Hotel**, there is an efficient centre, manned by Hong Kong Chinese and local staff. It has a comprehensive range of facilities and is open 9 am—10 pm (last booking is 8 pm for cable, 9.30 pm for telex).

At the Garden, a Hong Kong-based company, **Sullivan's Secretaries** (tel. 338989 ext. 3194; fax. 3121), runs the business centre which is open Monday-Friday 8.30 am—6.30 pm, Saturday 9 am—5 pm (closed Sunday). During the trade fair it is open every day until 10 pm. A team of secretaries here are mostly recruited from expatriate wives.

The **White Swan** (tel. 886968; tlx. 44688) is setting up a more comprehensive centre. At the moment it is open 8 am—11.30 pm and is manned by local staff.

There are two meeting rooms for hire. A room for six to eight people costs Rmb150 for eight hours and a room for 10—12 people costs Rmb250.

Canton's **World Trade Center Club** (Rooms 834—7 Garden Hotel; tel. 332899 ext. 7834-7837; tlx. 44526; cable 4735) promises to be another useful service for business travellers. WTC Canton is one of World Trade Center's 118 offices throughout the world. In addition to its normal service to WTC members, it will provide secretarial services to non-members — at a lower cost than at Sullivan's. WTC also arranges invitations in advance for the trade fair and can get passes issued on arrival for the increasing number of foreign businessmen who turn up on spec.

The organization has a liaison office in the Dongfang Hotel to arrange contacts with the **Guangzhou Foreign and Economic Affairs Centre** (tel. 669900, tlx. 44439). This centre includes all the major Chinese organizations which foreign businessmen may need to contact, including the Canton branch of Mofert (Ministry of Foreign Economic Relations and Trade), banks, lawyers and accountants.

Praxis Commercial Services (China Hotel, Office Tower Room 1358—9; tel. 663388; tlx. 44292; fax. 1358) is a joint venture which originally provided services solely for the oil companies. Services include contract registration, customs clearance, car or van hire, setting up meetings and arranging tours.

Sights of Canton

The city of Canton, or Guangzhou as it is now officially written, is about 112 kilometres (70 miles) from the South China Sea at the apex of the Pearl River delta. With a population of over three million, it is the capital, commercial centre, and major port of Guangdong Province.

The newest part of Canton lies south of the Pearl River and consists of industrial suburbs. North of the river are broad avenues of shops, offices, and hotels, with several attractive landscaped gardens and parks. Stretching away to the northeast are the foothills of Baiyun Mountain.

The basis of modern Canton dates from the 1920s, when the waterfront was cleared of its notorious floating brothels, and its squalid slums were levelled to make way for tree-lined boulevards and parks.

New highrise blocks have spring up everywhere over the past seven or eight years — office blocks, hotels, apartments — but the characteristic buildings are four or five storeys high with street-level arcades reminiscent of old sections of Hong Kong and Southeast Asian Chinatowns.

The city is roughly divided into four sections. The east-west Zhongshan Lu is bisected by Jiefang Lu which runs north from the river near Haizhu Guangchang (Haizhu Square) to the Trade Fair Exhibition Hall.

Canton does not offer the majestic architecture of Beijing or the gardens of Suzhou or ancient tombs of Xi'an. But it has always been a trading centre with pragmatic attitudes, and the city has attractions for all visitors. There are of course reminders of the 19th-century foreign settlement in the old mansions of Shamian Island, the Roman Catholic cathedral, and the waterfront business houses. There are memorials to Canton's revolutionary tradition and a handful of interesting temples.

Temple of the Six Banyan Trees

The Temple of the Six Banyan Trees (Liurongsi) was founded in the fifth century, later suffered devastation by fire, and was rebuilt under the Song during the 11th century. Its outstanding feature is a 60-metre (196-foot) tall pagoda, known as the Flowery Pagoda (Huata) because of its variegated appearance. The pagoda has nine exterior and 17 interior storeys that can be ascended by stairs, offering an excellent view of the entire temple grounds and the broad extent of the city. Looking south it is possible to pick out the plain grey minaret of the Huaisheng Mosque (see page 82). This minaret is known as the Naked Pagoda (Guangta) as opposed to the ornate Buddhist Huata.

The Temple of the Six Banyan Trees has been a Zen temple since the Tang Dynasty (618–907), patronized by followers of Huineng, the Sixth Patriarch. It remains so today and is the centre of the Canton Buddhist Association. A community of monks is in residence.

The name of the temple is linked to a story from the Song Dynasty. In the year 1100 the celebrated scholar, calligrapher and poet Su Dongpo arrived at the temple and was delighted by six banyan trees in the courtyard.

Buddhist patriarch

Inspired by this sight he wrote two large Chinese characters, *liu rong*, meaning six banyans. It has kept the name ever since. To the left, between the temple's entrance and the pagoda, is a corridor of stone tablets that recount events in the history of the temple. Among these is a tablet with Su Dongpo's two famous characters deeply engraved.

Several buildings of the temple have been restored over the past six years and are in active use. Most important of these is a large hall directly behind the pagoda that houses three large statues of the Buddha (five tonnes each) and one of Guanyin, the Goddess of Mercy. All are made of brass and were cast in 1663 during the Qing Dynasty. There is a bronze statue of Huineng to the south of the pagoda cast nearly a thousand years ago in 989.

The temple is open daily 8 am–5.30 pm.

Guangxiao Temple

Guangxiao Temple, founded at the end of the fourth century, is one of the oldest structures in Canton. Local people know the saying that roughly translates 'Before there was Goat City (Canton), first there was Guangxiao'. The temple was a regular destination of monks from India who came to China to lecture, spread Buddhism and supervise scriptural translations.

In 676 Huineng was tonsured and initiated into the monkhood here. He became the Sixth Patriarch of Zen Buddhism and leader of the Southern School, propounding the doctrine of sudden rather than gradual enlightenment.

Over the centuries Guangxiao Temple has been damaged and repaired many times, most recently in the 1950s, resulting in a hybrid style. Nevertheless, the principal architectural features are from the Southern Song (1127–1279), most clearly seen in the Great Hall. The large rectangular shape, the brownish-red colour and broad eaves give a feeling of amplitude and generosity to the whole building. The interior columns are shaped like silk shuttles and the rafters designed to be half the height of these pillars. The high roof and open plan give relief from heat and humidity and allow typhoon winds to pass through without causing any damage.

Directly behind the Great Hall is an octagonal stone pagoda. This is the Pagoda of the Sixth Patriarch's Hair, so named because, according to legend, it sprouted from the spot where Huineng buried his hair after being tonsured.

The most precious extant structure within the grounds of Guangxiao Temple is an iron pagoda near the eastern wall. It was constructed in 967 at another temple and moved here around 1235. Its square, seven-tiered design, fine decoration and good condition make it an important relic. A similar, though damaged, pagoda stands at the western wall.

The attractive temple grounds, tended by the monks in residence, have a number of handsome trees amidst many small pavilions and halls. A small nursery sells *bonsai* and other plants. An annexe at the entrance to the temple houses an antique shop that sells a selection of paintings, porcelain, statuary, jewellery and knick-knacks.

The temple entrance is down a small street, Guangxiao Lu, off busy Renmin Lu. It is open 8 am–5 pm.

Chen Family Temple

The Chen Family Temple (Chenjiasi) was built between 1890 and 1894. It is remarkable for its enormous size, its combination of building materials, and its ornate glazed pottery.

The surname 'Chen' is extremely common in Guangdong; Chens from 72 counties around the province contributed money and material to build the temple and participate in its two primary functions of ancestor veneration and education. The temple is often referred to as the Chen Family School.

Inspection of nearly any part of the temple will reveal intricate and exquisite carving in wood, brick, stone, lime and pottery. These display fans and flutes, courtesans and palanquins, birds and beasts, in short all aspects and objects of a rich, happy existence. There are also ornamental iron castings.

The showpiece is a rambling, dazzling section of glazed pottery sculpture that runs 28 metres (92 feet) along the roof. It depicts characters and stories from Chinese mythology and historical legends.

The ground plan of the temple complex is carefully designed and divided into sections of three. Two 'clear cloud corridors' function as the dividers, running from the left and right of the entrance all the way to the back hall of the temple. There are nine halls altogether, formed by three ranks of three, each separated by an open courtyard.

The central hall at the back of the temple has an elaborate shrine and a table altar of genuine gold leaf. In former times thousands of tablets commemorating Chen relatives would be stacked around the altar.

In a room at the left of the temple is a small museum showing pottery objects from Neolithic times up to the Qing but no information on the exhibits is given in English. This is just a small part of the much larger collection donated to China by Yang Quan, a wealthy gentleman from Hong Kong.

The temple functions today as an exhibition ground and museum of art and architecture.

Huaisheng Mosque and Guangtasi

Four early mosques were built in China; the oldest is here in Canton. The other three are in Quanzhou, Fujian Province; in Hangzhou, Zhejiang Province; and the last at Yangzhou in Jiangsu Province.

Huaisheng Mosque (Huaisheng Qingzhensi) was constructed in the early years of the Tang Dynasty, around 650. It was built as an outpost of Islam and was the religious and cultural centre of Arab merchants. The Pearl River was much broader in those days, the north bank reaching right to the front of the mosque, and it is said that these merchants sailed here directly upon reaching Canton to give thanks for the safe voyage.

The mosque entrance is on Guangta Lu through small gates, but entry may be refused to non-Moslems, particularly on Fridays. Its minaret, Guangta, can be ascended by two circular stairways, each 153 steps, that cling to the interior of the tower. From the top of the minaret there is an excellent view of the whole city. Notice that three great landmarks, the Buddhist Flowery Pagoda at the Temple of the Six Banyan Trees, the Moslem minaret, and the spires of the Catholic cathedral form a single straight north to south axis.

The gate-tower at the entrance was rebuilt during Emperor Kangxi's reign (1662−1722) on Tang-Dynasty remains. It retains the Tang style.

The Kanyuelou (Tower For Watching the Moon) stands between the entrance and main prayer hall. It was used as an observation point to watch the moon's changes for plotting the lunar calendar. The main prayer hall was fully refurbished in 1935 on the basis of Ming-Dynasty style.

Abbey Wangus, the reputed uncle of Mohammed, is the commemorated saint who came to China as an Islamic missionary in the seventh century (see below).

The gardens and courtyard are pleasing and peaceful, surrounded by a high wall. A sitting room near the base of the minaret is used for greeting and entertaining visitors. Many delegations come to this mosque from Malaysia, Pakistan and Arab countries and it serves the sizeable local Moslem community which includes a steady stream of traders from Xinjiang and northern China.

There is a small library behind the main prayer hall with pictures of Mecca, Medina and Jerusalem.

Ancient Tomb of the Islamic Saint

In the northern part of the city, hidden away amidst trees and thick overgrowth, is a remarkable tomb (Qingzhen Xianxian Gumu), more than 1,300 years old. It was built by the Moslems of Canton to honour Abbey Wangus, a zealous missionary who reputedly came to China at Mohammed's instruction.

The tomb is a squat, square structure with thick walls and a half-dome roof topped with a red onion-shaped decoration. The Arabian-style tomb is the seventh century original. There is a memorial arch inscribed with 'the Highest Moral' beyond which is the entrance to the coffin chamber. Inside, the coffin is covered with red and yellow silk and a large red satin cloth.

Surrounding the main tomb of Abbey Wangus are dozens of smaller tombs of imams, all within a high, walled compound. The whole complex has recently been restored, and the entrance gates are kept locked. Entry may be refused without prior appointment.

Before reaching the tombs there is a cluster of Ming-Dynasty buildings. In one of these, to the left of the main entrance, is a fascinating map carved in stone, dated 1925. It shows the huge extent of the Moslem community and its holdings at the time, now taken over by roads, a gymnasium, offices and public housing.

It is difficult to find this site and many local people do not know its location. It is just north of the Canton Gymnasium, abutting the Lanhua Orchid Exhibition gardens. A small road goes past the entrance to the garden; follow it until you reach a dead end. To the right there is a path of flat stones that will lead you to the tomb's main gate, on the left, after a five-minute walk.

Roman Catholic Cathedral

Begun in 1860 and consecrated in 1863, the cathedral was built in Neo-Gothic style and is a prominent landmark located just off Yanjiang Lu in Laodong Lu. The foundation stones on the east and west sides of the church are engraved in Latin: 'Rome' and 'Jerusalem'.

The structure, with its twin spires, was designed by a celebrated French architect and built entirely of granite. Consequently it is referred to in Chinese as the Stone House (Shishi). Its English name is now Sacred Heart of Jesus Church.

For many years used as a warehouse, it is now again open to worshippers. The interior, which was stripped bare, is gradually being restored. Mass is celebrated twice each morning and more frequently on Sundays and on public holidays; a notice in English inside the cathedral gives details of times.

Mausoleum of the 72 Martyrs

Prior to the Republican revolution of 10 October 1911, numerous armed uprisings were launched to bring down the Qing government and end dynastic rule forever. Under the guidance of Sun Yatsen, the revolutionaries fomented revolt at many sites in south China.

The most famous of these insurrections took place on 27 April 1911. It became known as the Battle of Canton and was intended to attack the office of the Qing governor. The uprising failed and more than one hundred young revolutionaries died, but only 72 of the bodies could be retrieved and buried together.

The Mausoleum of the 72 Martyrs (Qishier Lieshimu) was built as a memorial in 1918. Donations came largely from overseas Chinese through branches of the China Nationalist League. Some contributions arrived from as far away as Moose Jaw, Canada and Antofagasta, Chile.

Underlying the political and memorial motives for building the mausoleum there is a curious blending of Buddhist, Greek, Egyptian and Chinese symbolism. A Statue of Liberty stands with torch and tablet. There are an Egyptian-style obelisk and Chinese guardian lions. Buddhist motifs of lotus flowers, *vajras*, *dharma* wheels and swastikas are present in many stone carvings.

The mausoleum lies within an area known as Huanghuagang or Yellow Flower Hill, a park with gardens and wooded areas.

Peasant Movement Institute

One of the most significant and attractive memorials to the founders of China's Communist Party is the Institute where, in July 1924, Mao Zedong and his comrades began teaching their doctrine. It closed in 1927 with the failure of the Canton Commune.

The Institute (Nongmin Yundong Jiangxisuo), which was devoted to teaching young cadres, was one of the first schools of communism in China. Mao Zedong lectured here on 'the problem of the Chinese', 'rural education' and 'geography' and expounded his highly influential 'analysis of classes in Chinese society'.

The institute was housed in a 16th-century Ming temple of Confucius with a superb roof sporting glazed ceramic animals. The interior has been restored to its 1925 style, with simple dormitories for the students, a refectory, classrooms and Mao's office, complete with desk, wire in-trays and pen holders, and bedroom. The austere, almost monastic, environment helped to shape China's modern revolutionary leaders and is symbolic of their desire for a simple, disciplined society. Documents and photographs relating to the early years of the Communist Party are on display.

There are signs and explanations in English for some items at the Institute (open 8.45 am−5 pm). Entry is at 42 Zhongshan Si Lu.

Memorial Park to the Martyrs of the Canton Uprising

When the Canton Commune was crushed in mid-December 1927 by the Guomindang (the Nationalists), more than 5,000 revolutionaries were killed. Their remains are now contained in a large tumulus set in a pleasant park (Guangzhou Qiyi Lieshi Lingyuan). It has a boating lake, islands, and large stone book carved with calligraphy by Zhou Enlai. A remarkable chrysanthemum exhibition is held in the park each autumn and there are other seasonable flower shows.

To the east of martyrs' tomb are two pavilions, built to commemorate Soviet consular officials and Koreans who died in the uprising. Each has the slightly macabre title of Pavilion of Blood-Cemented Friendship. Entry to the park is on Zhongshan San Lu.

Sun Yatsen Memorial Hall

A little south of Yuexiu Park in Dongfeng Zhong Lu is the city's major monument to Sun Yatsen (Zhongshan Jiniantang), who led the 1911 Revolution to overthrow the Manchu Empire. It was built in 1925 in strong Chinese traditional style without interior columns and consists of an entrance hall and a large pavilion-shaped tower, covered with brilliant blue tiles. The tiles were specially made at the ceramic centre of Shiwan near Foshan (see page 95) and replaced during extensive repairs in 1963. Inside is a 5,000-seat theatre mostly used for variety and drama performances. A bronze statue of Dr Sun Yatsen stands in front of the hall. It is possible to go into the auditorium during the day and wander on the surrounding lawns (open 8 am−5 pm).

Lu Xun Museum

Part of the former site of Sun Yatsen University is now devoted to a collection of books, pamphlets and memorabilia of Lu Xun (Lu Xun Bowuguan), the most famous writer of modern China. He came south to Canton from Amoy (Xiamen) to take up the positions of director and dean of the Literary College in January 1927.

Though he spent less than a year at Sun Yatsen University, the months in Canton, surrounded by intellectual and revolutionary activity, were important for his subsequent thinking and writing. Unfortunately none of the exhibits have English-language explanations. Entrance is through large gates on Dezheng Bei Lu (open 8 am-noon, 2.30 pm−5.30 pm).

Shamian Island

The British and French obtained concessions on this island, originally nothing more than a sandbank, in 1859. Canton was the focus of the first Opium War and the Europeans had been pressing the Chinese to grant them a territorial base for the previous 16 years.

This enclave of 18 hectares (44 acres) was linked to the shore by two bridges which were closed at 10 pm each night. Feeling safe from attack, the foreigners built a small European world of stately mansions, churches, embassies, banks, tennis courts, a yacht club, a football pitch and the Victoria Hotel.

By 1911 there were over 300 residents from Britain, the USA, France, Holland, Italy, Germany, Portugal and Japan. In the 1920s Shamian was attacked by local revolutionaries but the settlement survived until the Revolution of 1949.

After the communist takeover, the mansions became government offices or run-down apartment houses and the Catholic church was

used as a printing factory. But in recent years repair work on at least some of the office buildings has prevented complete decay. The Catholic church, Our Lady of Lourdes Church, has reopened, and mass is held on Sundays at 6.30 am and 7.30 am. The times of other services should be checked in the church.

Shamian Island has become a favourite haunt of foreign backpackers. Small street cafés, simple restaurants, and bicycle-hire shops have sprung up round the Guangzhou Youth Hostel. At the other end of the hotel spectrum, the deluxe White Swan Hotel, opened in 1982, towers above the island's older buildings. Despite roadworks and construction projects, Shamian Island remains a relative oasis of tranquility, where citizens and visitors can stroll along the broad avenues shaded by giant banyan trees.

Qingping Market

Just north of Shamian lies the large Qingping market, famous for the wide variety of wildlife on sale, including at least one endangered species — the pangolin. Other culinary delicacies are civet cat (some looking remarkably like the domestic cat), dog, snake and owl.

Farmers from all corners of the province bring their produce to this noisy, crowded market. It spreads through several streets, and, if the wildlife is not to your taste, there are plenty of interesting streets selling a huge range of vegetables, flowers, Chinese medicines, dried foods and fish. It is busiest in the morning, although there is plenty of activity throughout the day.

South China Botanical Garden

This superb botanical garden (Huanan Zhiwuyuan), the largest in China, is located to the northeast of Canton beyond the suburb of Shahe. It was established in 1958 and is administered by the Chinese Academy of Sciences. The purpose of the garden is three-fold: to conduct research, promote appreciation and popular knowledge of botany, and to present a beautiful, lush setting for public enjoyment. Visitors will find it a cool haven of peace from the city. It is best to visit on a weekday to avoid the weekend crowds, but the garden is large enough for a quiet spot to be found at any time.

Two and a half leisurely hours are needed to see the main parts of the garden. It is divided into sections, each with its own focus and characteristics. There are special areas devoted to palms, economically important plants, bamboo, conifers, ornamental trees and precious relic plants — living fossils from an earlier age — such as the Chinese cypress (*Glyptostrobus pensilis*).

The greenhouse section is not extensive but well kept and a good place to see exotic species from around China and the world. South China Botanical Garden has established programmes of exchange with 60 foreign countries.

There is a teahouse for refreshments set amidst shady trees on the edge of a small lake. The botanical garden is open 8 am−5 pm each day and can be reached by bus number 28 from Shahe, a 20-minute taxi-ride from Canton.

Yuexiu Park and the Canton Municipal Museum

Canton's most famous park spreads 100 hectares (247 acres) east of the Trade Fair Exhibition Hall in the north part of the city. Yuexiu Park (Yuexiu Gongyuan) features landscaped gardens, three boating lakes with islands accessible by humpbacked bridges, and quiet walks. It also contains a stadium which can hold 30,000 people, an Olympic-sized swimming pool, and other pools.

The outstanding feature of the park is the five-storey **Zhenhai Tower** (Zhenhailou), built in 1380 and rebuilt as a watchtower in 1686. Today the tower houses the Canton Municipal Museum (Guangzhou Bowuguan). Each floor is devoted to different aspects of Canton's history. The museum is open daily 8.30 am−5.30 pm. But no English-language signs are provided.

The ground floor displays maps and diagrams of the city and important surrounding sites. Here also is the museum shop that sells historical publications, reproductions, paintings and craft items. The first floor has some prehistoric tools but shows primarily objects from the Han Dynasty (206 BC−AD 220). Among these the best are pottery tomb figurines of animals, farm scenes and whimsical, distorted human characters.

The second floor covers the Sui (581−618), Tang (618−907) and Song (960−1279) Dynasties. Next to a small exhibit of the Huaisheng Mosque there are two wonderful glazed ceramic pieces from the Tang. They are of Arab traders with large, beaked noses, foreign and bizarre to Chinese eyes.

The third floor belongs to the Ming and Qing. It shows primarily the development of science and industry in Canton. There is a good display of 18th-century clocks; and other sections on this floor are devoted to the early anti-imperialist movements.

The top floor focuses on revolutionary history and the lives of important leaders such as Kang Youwei and Sun Yatsen. It is striking how broad a role the city of Canton and local people played in the past hundred years of China's history.

In front of the museum stands a row of steles that recount aspects of Canton's history. A number of cannons point their muzzles towards the city; one of them is inscribed 'F. Krupp 1867'.

Statue of the Five Goats

On a hill in Yuexiu Park is the much photographed 20th-century statue of five goats (Wuyang Suxiang) which, according to legend, brought five heavenly messengers to Canton with gifts of cereals for the inhabitants of the area. The goats have been adopted as official symbols of the city. Although they have little artistic merit, it is a pleasant walk up to see them.

Baiyun Mountain

On the northeast edge of Canton, 15 kilometres (9 miles) from the centre of the city is Baiyunshan, or White Cloud Mountain, a resort and cool retreat for residents and visitors. Spreading over 72 square kilometres (28 square miles), its highest point is 427 metres (1,400 feet). Winding roads to the top offer superb views of Canton and the Pearl River delta. At intervals there are belvederes with teahouses.

Canton's Parks

The **Orchid Garden** (Lan Pu), located down a narrow lane off Jiefang Bei Lu, opposite the entrance to Yuexiu Park, is a quiet retreat with thick groves of bamboo, shaded paths, rockeries and a traditional teahouse beside a lily pond filled with carp. The orchid house claims to have over 100 varieties. Entry is Rmb2, which entitles you to tea at the teahouse. The relatively hefty entrance fee keeps out the crowds, making this a delightful spot to spend time away from the general bustle of the city. It is open daily 8 am−6 pm.

One of the most attractive features of Canton's parks are their many small lakes, where it is possible to hire boats. Especially worth visiting are **Liuhua Park** (Liuhua Gongyuan), within easy walking distance of the Dongfang Hotel, **Dongshan Lake Park** (Dongshanhu Gongyuan) on the banks of the Pearl River to the east of the city, and the **Liwan Park** (Liwan Gongyuan) on the western edge of Canton.

The busiest park in the city is the **Cultural Park** (Wenhua Gongyuan), behind the Renmin Mansion and the Nanfang Department Store. It is a playground for all the family, with a roller-skating rink, fairground rides, an open air theatre and cinema, exhibition halls and teahouses.

Canton's **Zoo** is also set in a large park off Xianlie Lu. An attractive zoo, it has over 200 species, including four pandas.

Canton's Factories, 1769

William Hickey, an employee of the East India Company, visited Canton during the winter of 1769–80. He recorded his impressions of life in the 'factories' (where the foreign traders were based) in his diary:

'About half a mile above the City suburbs, in going from Whampoa, is a wharf, or embankment, regularly built of brick and mortar, extending more than half a mile in length, upon which wharf stands the different factories or places of residence of the Supercargoes, each factory having the flag of its nation on a lofty ensign staff before it. At the time I was in China they stood in the following order. First, the Dutch, then, the French, the English, the Swedes, and last, the Danes. Each of these factories, besides admirable banqueting, or public rooms for eating, &c., have attached to them sets of chambers, varying in size according to the establishment. The English being far more numerous than any other nation trading with China, their range of buildings is much the most extensive. Each supercargo has four handsome rooms; the public apartments are in front looking to the river; the others go inland to the depth of two or three hundred feet, in broad courts, having the sets of rooms on each side, every set having a distinct and separate entrance with a small garden, and every sort of convenience. Besides the factories which belong to the East India Company there are also others, the property of Chinese, who let them to European and Country Captains of ships, merchants and strangers whom business brings to Canton. For several years there has been an Imperial flag flying before a factory occupied by the Germans. The Americans (whom the Chinese distinguish by the expressive title of second chop Englishmen) have also a flag. The number of supercargoes employed by the East India Company in the year 1769 was twelve, but when we arrived there were only eleven resident, one being in Europe for recovery of his health.'

The port of Canton, 19th century

Foshan

The most frequent excursion from Canton made by foreign visitors has been to Foshan, a city just 20 kilometres (12.5 miles) southwest of Canton, although there are now other open towns in the province which are more interesting.

A new highway is being built between Canton and Foshan, but for the moment traffic on the road is very heavy, and the short distance can take one and a half hours by taxi. The drive can no longer be recommended for a glimpse of Guangdong's rural life: new light industrial factories, and residential apartments are springing up along the road. A new fast train service to Foshan has been introduced — leaving early in the morning from the main railway station. Buses for Foshan leave from the main bus terminal in the southwest of the city.

Foshan's history goes back over 1,200 years, when Foshan (which means Buddha Hill) was an important religious centre frequently visited by monks from India. Foshan has always been known for its crafts; its pottery was famous in the Song Dynasty (960–1279), and during the Ming (1368–1644) local metalwork was among the most sophisticated in China. Five hundred years ago the economy of Foshan was so fully developed it was considered one of the four great Chinese market towns.

By the 18th century Foshan had a population of over a million people making it perhaps the largest city in the world at that time. Now, with over 300,000 inhabitants, Foshan remains an important industrial city with the traditional craft of pottery still a major industry. Its recent success in light industry has made it one of the richest towns in Guangdong. Evidence of its newfound wealth is demonstrated in the large number of buildings and roads under construction in the town, along with new hotels for local and Hong Kong Chinese businessmen.

The southern part of the town, with its bright ornamental traditional architecture, is a good place to explore on foot.

Many of Foshan's temples have fallen into decay, the **Daoist Ancestral Temple** (Zu Miao) with its highly decorated Qing buildings, ornate ceramic roofs, gilded wooden columns, Buddhist statues and Daoist sages is worth visiting. There is also a small museum, though no captions are in English. The temple complex has become a noisy recreation centre for China's domestic tourists, with bumper cars, souvenir shops, and a boisterous Chinese restaurant. Inside the temple buildings, the statues have been regilded, and the ceramics cleaned up. The temple is open 8.30 am–4.45 pm.

The former **Renshou Temple** (Renshousi) has been converted into a folk art centre where local craftsmen carry on age-old practices. The artists are used to foreign visitors flocking through their studios, and this is a good place to watch them at work. Papercuts with multiple layers of colour and gold paper is a special tradition, along with fishbones carving and the making of elaborate Chinese lanterns. Painters and calligraphers also produce poems and worthy works of art. Handicrafts and paintings are available for purchase, and the centre is open 8 am–6 pm.

Six kilometres (four miles) from the Ancestral Temple is the suburb of **Shiwan**, known as 'the pottery capital of south China'. It has churned out ceramic pieces of high artistic and practical quality since the 11th century, and today produces four categories of objects: birds and animals, figurines, miniature landscapes, and household items. All these are for sale in a vast showroom at the **Shiwan Artistic Ceramics Factory** (Shiwan Meishu Taocichang), where it is also possible to walk round and watch each phase of the work in progress. Prices for pottery range from a few yuan to over a thousand for an intricate 12-inch figure. Figures in the characteristic Shiwan reddish-brown glaze can be as much as Rmb7,000. A visit to the factory has been a standard component of CITS tours for the past ten years, but casual visitors are also welcome.

Hotels in Foshan

Foshan Guesthouse
75 Fenjiang Nan Lu
tel. 87923
tlx. 44773

佛山宾馆
汾江南路75号

Double rooms Rmb100 (new wing); Rmb75 (old wing); suites Rmb170, 300

A new wing, built through joint-venture with Hong Kong, has improved the standard of facilities at this CITS-run hotel. The hotel has IDD telephones, meeting rooms, telex and photocopy machines, as well as a small swimming pool, health centre, banquet room, bar and Western and Chinese restaurants.

Overseas Chinese Mansion (Huaqiao Dasha)
Zumiao Lu
tel. 86511
cable 4428

华侨大厦
祖庙路

Double rooms Rmb50, 60, 70

Directly opposite Renshou Temple Folk Art Centre, this hotel has recently been renovated. Guests are predominantly local and Hong Kong Chinese, and few of the staff speak English.

Rotating Palace Hotel (Xuangong Jiudian)
Zumiao Lu
tel. 85622
tlx. 44804
fax. 85622 ext. 328

旋宫酒店
祖庙路

Double rooms Rmb85, 100

This joint-venture hotel takes its name from its revolving top-floor restaurant. Facilities are middle range, with a fully-equipped business centre, and Chinese and Western food.

Foshan papercut

Zhaoqing

Zhaoqing is one the most popular scenic spots in Guangdong, though its limestone crags are not as spectacular as those in the Guilin area and the city lacks the character of those in the north of the province.

Zhaoqing lies 111 kilometres (63 miles) west of Canton. With its traditional name as Duanzhou, it is a city with over 2,000 years of history. The Song-Dynasty city walls can still be found within walking distance of the harbour. The West River (Xijiang) runs through the south of the city. Narrow streets near the river form the most interesting part of what is mainly a functional, modern city.

The two famous beauty spots of Zhaoqing are Seven Star Crags and Mount Dinghu just outside the city, 18 kilometres (11 miles) north of Zhaoqing.

Getting to Zhaoqing

By Road There is an airconditioned through-coach service between Hong Kong and Zhaoqing. The distance is 324 kilometres (202 miles) and the fare is HK$70. Airconditioned coaches between Shenzhen and Zhaoqing leave Shenchen at 9 am (Rmb16). Buses to Zhaoqing leave Canton from Yide Xi Lu at 8.10 am, 9.45 am and 10.45 am (Rmb7.60); the journey takes about three hours. Public buses are also available from Canton (at the bus station opposite the railway station), Shunde, Zhanjiang, Foshan and Taishan at least once a day.

There is a public bus service from Canton to Dinghu (96 kilometres or 60 miles) everyday. Buses and minibuses run frequently between Zhaoqing and Dinghu.

By Boat You can travel from Hong Kong to Zhaoqing along the West River by boat. There is also a ferry from the Dashatou Passenger Transport Station in Canton which departs every evening at 8 pm and arrive in Zhaoqing at 4 am. There are boats from Wuzhou (173 kilometres or 108 miles) and Jiangmen (127 kilometres or 79 miles) to Zhaoqing every day.

A number of Hong Kong-based agents, including CITS, run a variety of short tours that involve an overnight in Zhaoqing. The Garden Hotel and the Overseas Chinese Mansion in Canton also offer tours.

Hotels in the Zhaoqing Area

Furong Guesthouse
Duanzhou Liu Lu
Zhaoqing
tel. 23228

芙蓉宾馆
端洲六路

Double rooms with airconditioning US$26, without airconditioning US$13

This hotel, opened in 1981, is situated in the suburbs of Zhaoqing not far from Seven Star Crags. There are gardens, a restaurant and coffee shop.

Overseas Chinese Mansion (Huaqiao Dasha)
90 Tianning Bei Lu
Zhaoqing
tel. 22952

华侨大厦
天宁北路90号

Double rooms US$31−56

This highrise building opposite the main entry to Seven Star Crags was built in 1982 but has been refurbished and extended. There are Chiu Chow and Cantonese restaurants as well as a coffee shop and shop. Tickets for the airconditioned bus to Canton are on sale at the gate.

Duanzhou Hotel
Tianning Bei Lu
Zhaoqing
tel. 23215

端洲饭店
天宁北路

Double rooms Rmb43

This hotel is used mostly for overseas Chinese visitors. If you cannot speak Chinese the staff are likely to redirect you to the Overseas Chinese Hotel next door.

Songtao Guesthouse
Seven Star Crags
Resort
tel. 24412
cable 9038

松涛宾馆
七星岩风景区

Double rooms Rmb91, 114

The beautiful location, good service and facilities of this recently renovated hotel have made it the most popular in Zhaoqing. It is situated between two crags, Stone Palm and Toad, overlooking Central Lake (Zhongxinhu Lake). It has a good Chinese restaurant, a coffee shop, shops and a nightclub. The restaurant is the only one in Zhaoqing to have a menu in English. Tickets for the ferry and buses to Hongkong and Canton can be bought here. Minibuses run from the hotel to the town centre and to Dinghu. All rooms have airconditioning, a bathroom, TV and refrigerator.

**Star Lake Guesthouse
(Xinghu Binguan)**
Seven Star Crags
Resort

星湖宾馆
七星岩风景区

Double rooms Rmb26

This old hotel set in woods above Central
Lake offers friendly service and simple but
comfortable accommodation. There is a shop
and a restaurant. Rooms have a bathroom and
airconditioning.

**Bohai Lou
Guesthouse**
Seven Star Crags
Resort

波海楼
七星岩风景区

Double rooms Rmb24

This is another fine old building with about 40
rooms. It is situated to the west end of Seven
Star Crags, overlooking Central and Bohai
Lakes.

**Dinghu Travel
Service Guesthouse**

鼎湖旅社宾馆
鼎湖山

Double rooms Rmb20, 25

At the foothill of Mount Dinghu, this basic
hotel has 26 rooms with no airconditioning.

Gateway to Seven Star Crags

Sights of Zhaoqing

Seven Star Crags

Seven Star Crags is said to combine the tranquility of the West Lake in Hangzhou with the drama of the peaks and caverns of Guilin. Attractive it may be, but it is not as spectacular as either those places.

Seven limestone crags arranged in the shape of the Big Dipper (Ursa Major) give their name to this beauty spot in the suburbs of Zhaoqing. In 1636 the place became known as Star Lake (Xinghu Lake), though it had already been famous for its beauty as early as the Tang Dynasty (618−906). Over the past 1,000 years, numerous poems have been inscribed on the walls of the caves by poets and tourists.

Each crag is of different height and is given an evocative name — Lofty Wind, Jade Screen, Stone Chamber, Pillar of Heaven, Toad, Stone Palm and Hill Slope. Six artificial lakes have been created to surround the crags.

The area has been renovated and the stone-slab footpaths leading to the hilltops have been repaved. From the top of the crags you can enjoy a panoramic view of Zhaoqing and the West River. There are also a number of caverns famous for their stalactites and stalagmites.

Mount Dinghu

Mount Dinghu is 18 kilometres (11 miles) northeast of Zhaoqing. It is renowned for its beautiful scenery. It has officially been admitted to the World Nature Protection Association and is also one of the UNESCO ecology research centres. Areas west and south of Qingyun Temple have been closed to tourists, but there are still more than five scenic spots and pools where you can swim. The Buddhist **Qingyun Temple**, built in 1633, is known as one of the four famous monasteries of South China. A guesthouse within the temple complex offers simple dormitory accommodation (Rmb4 per bed). A travel service, shops, and a hotel have been established at the foot of the mountain.

Zhaoqing City

Within the city of Zhaoqing there are some places worth visiting. **Yuejiang Lou**, an impressive tower built on the banks of the Xi River in the Song Dynasty (960−1279), is also a memorial hall of the independent party of Ye Ting who fought in the 1925−7 civil war of China. Also by the river is the Ming-Dynasty **Chongxi Pagoda** built in 1582, worth climbing for the views of the town, river and crags. The Meian Nunnery (the Plum Nunnery), built during the Song Dynasty, now houses the **Zhaoqing Museum**.

Conghua Hot Springs

Once a luxurious spa for the rich, the hot springs resort of Conghua, 80 kilometres (50 miles) north of Canton, is now a popular vacation place for locals and visitors.

Clear, odourless, tasteless water from 12 sources bubbles up from the ground at temperatures of 30°–40°C (86°–104°F). The waters contain calcium, magnesium, potassium, sodium and silicon dioxide, and are proclaimed to be good for ameliorating arthritis, hypertension, neuralgia and other ailments.

Villas are scattered among the gardens and bamboo groves on either side of the Liuxi River. Water from the springs is piped directly into large private bathrooms in the hotels. There are also public baths built around hot springs on the east bank. Nearby is a small village with shops and restaurants.

About four kilometres (2.5 miles) away from the hot springs area, high in the hills, is the Heavenly Lake reservoir and a large waterfall. Several hotels and restaurants by the lake have recently been opened. Minibuses take you there from the hot spring resort (Rmb2).

The scenery around Conghua is not as spectacular as Guilin, but with green mountains on the near horizon and attractive parks, it is quietly beautiful. Thousands of lychee trees have been planted. The fruit is in season in mid summer. Other local specialities are Liuxi River green tea, honey and carved wood.

Getting to Conghua

The resort can be reached by public bus from Canton. There are buses throughout the day departing from the bus terminal at Baiyun Lu. The journey takes two and a half hours. Buses departing in the afternoon terminate in the town of Conghua. From here you must take a minibus to the hot springs resort.

CTS (HK) Ltd organizes several tours that include a night in Conghua in the itinerary, as does the Garden Hotel, Canton.

Hotels in Conghua

Cuixi Guesthouse
翠溪宾馆

Hubin Guesthouse
湖滨宾馆

Double rooms Rmb30–218

CITS owns this group of villa hotels. The most luxurious is Cuixi Guesthouse but all rooms have bathrooms with hot spring water. Rooms

**Pine Garden Hotel
(Songyuan Binguan)**
松园宾馆

**Hot Springs Hotel
(Wenquan Binguan)**
温泉宾馆

vary from a luxury suite to a simple but clean and comfortable three-bed room without airconditioning. The service at the Wenchuan restaurant, by the gates to these hotels, can be very slow. There is no menu in English.

Retired citizens in a cool temple courtyard

**Conghua Travel
Hotel (Conghua
Wenquan Luyou
Binguan)**
Conghua Hot Springs
Resort

从化温泉旅游宾馆
从化温泉风景区

Double rooms Rmb60

This new hotel, one of the first buildings you come to as you enter the resort, also has hot spring water piped to private bathrooms. Airconditioned buses to Canton leave from the hotel.

There are three hotels offering comfortable accommodation and airconditioned rooms for between Rmb 40 and 50 near the Heavenly Lake. These are Zuanshi Villa, Songping Villa and Tianhe Villa.

Hainan Island

The beautiful island of Hainan used to be regarded by the Chinese, emperors and communists alike, as nothing more than a place of exile, being the southern-most tip of the empire and thus suitably far away from Beijing. But now it is recognised for what it really is — a tropical paradise with enormous potential for tourism.

The authorities proudly call Hainan the Hawaii of China. Situated 50 kilometres (31 miles) off the southern tip of the Leizhou Peninsula, it lies on the same latitude as Hawaii and enjoys a similar warm, humid climate throughout the year. It has an annual average temperature of 26°C (78°F).

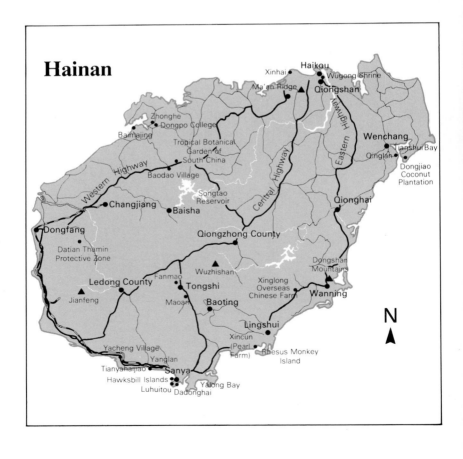

But while developing tourism is one of the main priorities for the island, it will be several years before it has the hotels and transportation network to qualify as a major holiday destination. In the meantime its gorgeous tropical beaches, which must be among the best in Southeast Asia, remain unspoilt and ready to be explored by those who want to get away from the crowds.

But there is more to Hainan than beaches. The lush mountainous interior is both beautiful and interesting culturally. For it is here that most of Hainan's minority peoples live — the Miao, Zhuang, and the Li who were the island's first inhabitants, arriving two thousand years ago. Hui (Moslems) make up the fourth minority group. Legend has it that this small community of 2,500 people was spawned by the crew of an Arab trading ship that went aground on a Hainan beach.

Hainan has a colourful, carefree atmosphere that is rare in China. In all the major towns there are large free markets with expansive arrays of fish, reptiles, mammals, fruits, vegetables and potions on sale. Also to be explored are small fishing villages where ancient skills of boat building and sail making can be seen.

Facilities for tourists have already been greatly improved. There is now an international-standard hotel in the northern city of Haikou, the island's capital. New hotels have opened or are due to open in Sanya, the southern regional centre and the city surrounded by Hainan's best beaches.

Roads between Haikou and Sanya, which lie 280 kilometres (175 miles) apart, have been upgraded. The three major routes, which run along the east of the island, through the central mountains and on the west side, link Haikou with all the important towns. The east and the central routes are more commonly used than the west, an area heavily fortified as a result of hostilities between China and neighbouring Vietnam. An international airport at Sanya is due to open in 1989.

Hainan is nearly as large as Taiwan but has a small population relative to the rest of China, with less than six million people. (Taiwan has a population approaching 20 million.) Now Beijing wants to develop Hainan's rich resources, using the once-backward island as a show-case of prosperity with which to woo Taiwan back into the Chinese fold. It is thus being made into an independent province and what is expected to be the most liberal Special Economic Zone in the People's Republic. As well as tourism, agriculture and fisheries are seen as the major areas of growth. The lush countryside already produces economically significant amounts of pepper, rubber, cocoa, coffee, tea, sisal, hardwoods, copra and fruit. But the greatest change may come if large deposits of oil are struck when drilling begins in the near future off the northern shores of the island.

Getting to Hainan

By Air There are now daily flights between Hong Kong and the island's main city of Haikou. There are seven CAAC flights a week and, on Wednesdays and Sundays, Dragonair flights (US$80 one way). There are 14 CAAC flights a week between Canton and Haikou (Rmb135) and there are two flights a month between Haikou and Singapore. By 1988 there will be several flights a week between Haikou and Beijing.

There are plans to build an international airport in Sanya, due for completion in 1989. In the meantime there are four flights a week between Canton and Sanya (Rmb 216 one way). The route is heavily booked and additional services are expected. There is likely to be an air shuttle service between Haikou and Sanya.

By Boat Haikou is accessible by boat from Hong Kong; departures are from Tai Kok Tsui pier about once a week taking 20 hours (US$20−48). Tickets can be bought at the Hong Kong CTS office (Queen's Road Central). From Canton there are also daily departures, (Rmb16.50−34.90), as well as from Zhanjiang (daily departures), Singapore and Penang. The ferry between Hong Kong and Haikou is comfortable, unlike the 26-hour journey from Canton. The journey can be rough during windy weather conditions. There is also a ferry between Hong Kong and Sanya, which runs twice a month (US$24−54).

By Bus There are frequent non-airconditioned buses everyday from the mainland city of Zhanjiang to the tip of the Leizhou peninsula, Hai'an. The journey takes about four hours. Haikou can then be reached by a two-hour trip on a crowded ferry across the Qiongzhou Strait. A connecting bus and boat ticket to Haikou from Zhanjiang costs around Rmb8. There are also airconditioned buses from Canton and Hong Kong but both journeys are very long.

Getting around Hainan

The best way to see the island is to take to its arterial highways, known as the eastern, central and western routes. The eastern route offers tropical scenery of coconut trees, beaches and fishing villages, while the central route takes you through the mountainous interior where the Li and Miao minority nationalities live. The western route is more remote and is still rarely taken by tourists. All three routes stretch from Haikou city in the north to Sanya in the south.

The easiest way to get around is to hire a four-wheel drive vehicle or van with a driver (Rmb200 a day), which can be organized through

Haikou Tower Hotel, the CTS office in the Overseas Chinese Hotel or the Nantian Hotel.

There are several airconditioned buses a day which take the eastern route to connect Haikou with Sanya as well as towns along the way — Wenchang, Qionghai, Wanning and Lingshui. The journey between Haikou and Sanya takes six hours and costs Rmb16.

Non-airconditioned buses link the central regional capital, Tongshi, with Haikou and Sanya. The journey from Haikou to Tongshi takes over five hours (Rmb7), and from Sanya two hours (Rmb4). Local buses connect all the major towns along the western route. There is also a 220-kilometre (138-mile) railway running from Zhanjiang to Sanya. Steam trains run infrequently. Minibuses bound for Tongshi leave from outside the Sanya Hotel (see page 120).

Within Haikou and Sanya there are small taxis. These do not have meters so beware of being overcharged. The journey from Haikou Tower Hotel to the town centre should not cost more than Rmb3. More fun are the 'Hainan rockets' — motorbikes with makeshift side-cars. The fare from the Dadonghai Hotel outside Sanya to the town centre is about Rmb4. Hainan rockets can be found in Haikou, Sanya and Tongshi.

Children at play, Hainan Island

Haikou

Situated at the northern tip of the island, Haikou is Hainan's economic and political hub. At present the city suffers from a serious lack of electricity because of a long drought that has limited the amount of water available for hydro-electric power. Buildings without their own generators at times only have electricity on one day a week. The power station — a series of converted train carriages — is well worth a look. A new power station is due to open in 1988. A number of interesting side-trips can be made from Haikou (see pages 114–115).

Hotels in Haikou

Haikou Tower Hotel (Haikou Taihua Jiudian)
Binhai Dadao
tel. 23990
tlx. 45050

海口泰华酒店
滨海大道

Double rooms US$30-$35; suite $154

This 240-room hotel, a joint venture with Hong Kong and situated on the Haikou waterfront, is the only international-class hotel on the island. It has Western and Chinese restaurants, both of which serve excellent food, and pool-side barbecues are organized regularly. Facilities include a swimming pool, tennis courts, shops and foreign exchange service. All rooms have colour televisions, refrigerators and IDD telephones. The hotel, which opened in 1986, is a major attraction within the town; its bar, disco and restaurants are the most popular nightspots among locals. The hotel's travel office can arrange transport and accommodation elsewhere on the island, and can organize waterskiing and scuba diving trips. Reservations can be made in Hong Kong through Tower Hotels Ltd, tel. 3-659003.

Overseas Chinese Mansion (Huaqiao Dasha)
17 Datong Lu
tel. 24523, 23623
tlx. 45039

华侨大厦
大同路17号

Double rooms Rmb50, Rmb58; without air-conditioning Rmb28; suites Rmb98

CTS has its office in this busy, recently renovated hotel. There are two Chinese restaurants, a Western coffee shop and a car-hire service.

Nantian Hotel
Haikou Jichang Xi
Lu
tel. 23880
cable 1235

南天宾馆
海口机场西路

*Double rooms Rmb70; suites Rmb120;
dormitory Rmb8*

This 177-room hotel was also opened in 1986.
All rooms have colour televisions, IDD
telephones and refrigerators. There are
Chinese and Western dining rooms, a dance
hall, shop, and taxi service. Tours of Hainan
can be arranged.

**Conference Hotel
(Qiongyuan Binguan)**
Haifu Lu
tel. 25245

琼园宾馆
海府路

Double room Rmb60

This was the hotel in a garden setting that
many foreign businessmen stayed in before
the opening of the Haikou Tower. It has a
coffee shop and two Chinese restaurants.

**Friendship Hotel
(Youyi Binguan)**
Datong Lu
tel. 24712

友谊宾馆
大同路

Double rooms Rmb50

The hotel has a good Chinese restaurant
serving local specialities. The chicken with
coconut and taro duck are worth a try.

Sights of Haikou

Wugong Shrine and the Memorial Temple of Su Dongpo

These are the most interesting historic sights near Haikou. Situated
about four kilometres (2.5 miles) southeast of Haikou in Fucheng
Township, the shrine, Wugongci, was established in honour of five
patriotic officials: Li Deyu of the Tang Dynasty, and Li Gang, Li
Guang, Zhao Ding and Hu Quan of the Song Dynasty. It was first
built in 1617 during the Ming Dynasty and was rebuilt in 1889 during
the Qing Dynasty. Apart from Li Deyu, who was banished to Hainan
after losing battles between rival political factions, the other four
officials were banished after being defeated by trickery.

The shrine has now been converted into a temple. In the Xuepu
Hall on the right is an 800-year-old Sakyamuni statue and the Hainan
Garrison Bell made in 1436. There is also a collection of brass drums.

Nearby is the memorial temple of Song poet Su Dongpo who was
banished to the area during a severe drought. Su Dongpo dug a well,
found within the temple complex, which is now known as the Millet
Spring.

The Tomb of Hairui

Hairui (1514−87) was born in Qiongshan, near Haikou. He was a politician in the Ming Dynasty, famous for his integrity and uprightness, but was jailed after falling out of favour with the emperor, Jiajing. His tomb is in the southwestern suburbs of Haikou and is surrounded by coconut trees, stone guards and horses. It can be reached by taxi, or by Hainan rocket.

Changdi Lu

Although Haikou has few noteworthy sights as such, there are several interesting areas to walk in. Changdi Lu is a colourful street which runs alongside the river. Dozens of fishing junks, most of which are still powered by sail, are moored here. The boats double as homes for the fishermen and their families.

Xinmin Lu Market

This large, daily market sells everything from exotic spices and tropical fruits to live pigs, snakes and fish. It is open all day, but is at its best in the morning.

Qiongtai Academy

The academy at Qiongtai is situated behind the backyard of Qiongtai Teachers' College, in the region of Qiongshan. It was established in 1710.

The academy can be reached by passing through the Teachers' College. This opens onto a courtyard surrounded by old, faded buildings, with a central hall in the middle of the open space. Tall trees and the quiet courtyard evoke a scholarly atmosphere. With permission one can visit the old academy library which has a large collection of Qing-Dynasty books.

Side-trips from Haikou

On the coast to the northwest of Haikou, about half an hour's drive away, lies **Xinhai Fishing Village**. The village is a time-capsule where, along the beach, boats are built using ancient methods to bend wood and drill holes. Numerous boats are moored close to the shore while others can be seen under full sail. Large numbers of tanned children will greet you here. There are two local buses to the village a day. CTS tours also visit the village.

One of the world's best preserved craters, **Ma'an Ridge**, lies ten kilometres (six miles) southwest of Haikou. There are some excellent views of the surrounding countryside and sea from the top of the 200,000 year-old crater. The area is now being developed as a tourist

site, with a restaurant and pavilions being built. The drive through
Hainan countryside alone makes the trip worthwhile.

This huge stretch of mangroves skirting the bay around Donghai
harbour is an area known as the Forest in the Sea. This is the **Dongzhai
Mangrove Nature Reserve** which covers 600 hectares (1,500 acres).

East-coast Route from Haikou to Sanya

Seventy-three kilometres (46 miles) southeast of Haikou, on the east
coast, is the fishing town of **Wenchang**, famous for its Wenchang
chicken and for its coconut palms. The village can be visited on a day-
trip from Haikou, or as a break on the journey towards Sanya.
Alternatively you can stay in Wenchang at the Kangle Hotel. The trip
from Haikou takes one and a half hours. There are frequent local
buses, as well as the airconditioned buses heading for Sanya.

At the tip of the peninsula to the southeast of Wenchang is the
Dongjiao Coconut Plantation. The plantation can be reached by ferry
from Qinglan, a half-hour journey from Wenchang by mini-bus or
local bus. Local buses leave from Taiping Bridge, a 20-minute walk
from the main bus station. At Dongjiao you can drink fresh coconut
water and see coconut carvings being made.

It is worth hiring a boat (Rmb20 return trip from Qinglan) to take you on from the plantation to the mouth of the estuary. Here there is an almost endless, deserted beach. There are large sandbanks and the water is shallow. During onshore winds, the water is not as clear as the waters in the south. There is also an excellent small restaurant — the Garden Seafood Restaurant — where you can eat first-class lobster and fish, and drink coconut water, beneath the palms.

Northeast of Wenchang is the large beach of Tianshui Bay, at the foot of Mount Tonghu. Southwest of Qinglan is Zhilan Bay beach.

Travelling south from Wenchang you reach the abundant seaweed cultivation grounds of **Qionghai County**, an area good for scuba diving.

South from Qionghai lies the east coast city of **Wanning**. Not far from here are the **Dongshan Mountains**, now being developed as a scenic spot. The mountains are known for their bizarre rock outcrops, as well as the cave temple of Huafeng where you can have your fortune told. There are plans to renovate other temples and open a hotel. The Kangle Hotel in Wanning is also due to open soon. Dongshan mutton is another well-known Hainan dish and Dongshan black sheep are reared on this range.

A 40-minute bus-ride from Wanning will take you to Xinglong, where the **Xinglong Overseas Chinese Farm** is situated. Originally built by returned overseas Chinese, the farm produces tropical fruits and crops such as pineapple, pepper, coffee and arece nut. The Hot Spring Guesthouse, situated in the farm, is a convenient place to spend the night if you want to break your journey to Sanya. The best rooms (double US$22) face two large spring pools — one hot, the other scorching. There are also cheaper rooms.

Further south from Wanning, in **Lingshui**, there are two interesting places worth visiting. The first is the **pearl farm** at **Xincun** fishing village. Besides looking at the cultured pearl industry, Xincun itself is a colourful village.

The second is **Rhesus Monkey Island** (Nanwan Hou Dao), situated on the shore opposite Xincun. It can be reached by a five-minute ferry-ride and then a short bus journey, or a 30-minute walk. This is the only rhesus monkey protection area in China and is home for more than 1,000 specimens which live on the mountain. Staff have domesticated two troops which they assemble for tourists, at 9 am and 4 pm, by whistling.

Xincun can be reached from Sanya by minibus, as well as public buses. Minibuses leave from the Dadonghai Tourist Centre and the Sanya Hotel in the mornings.

Sanya

Sanya, in Yaxian County, is the southern capital of Hainan. The town, closed to individual travellers until recently, is now at the heart of the area that has been earmarked for rapid tourist development. To east and west of the port town are beaches that match the best in Southeast Asia. The nearby central hills add a beautiful backdrop to the region.

Sanya has more to offer than beaches and scenery. The large free market is well worth wandering through, while a visit to the fishing port should not be missed. Here you can watch fishermen unload their catch which they sell — or barter for firewood — to large crowds waiting on the shore.

The number of tourists visiting Sanya is already stretching facilities to their limit. New hotels are being built within the town itself but at the moment there is only one hotel along the beach front, where the greatest demand for rooms is. Plans are underway to build more hotels but these are not likely to open for a couple of years. The most ambitious of these is a joint-venture complex at Yalong Bay, about 20 kilometres (12.5 miles) from Sanya.

Getting around Sanya

At present there is no CTS office in Sanya but the Dadonghai Tourist Centre organizes a minibus service to Rhesus Monkey Island and the End of the Earth Beach. Minibuses to these places, as well as to Tongshi, leave regularly from outside Sanya Hotel in the town. Bus tickets to Haikou are sold here as well as at Dadonghai and Xinya Hotel.

Hainan rockets are the best way of getting around. They can be found in the town and outside the hotels, but beware — they frequently break down. Bicycles can be hired from the Kangaroo Club and Luhuitou Restaurant outside the Luhuitou Guesthouse (see below).

Hotels in Sanya

Dadonghai Tourist Centre
Tel. 998
Cable 8888

大东海旅游中心

New building: airconditioned rooms, Rmb60 and 70; old building: room with bathroom, Rmb30; dormitory Rmb10.

Situated about five kilometres east of Sanya, this is at the moment the only hotel that fronts on to a beach. The complex is split into two sections. The new building has carpeted, airconditioned rooms, while the old building has more basic accommodation. Tents can also be rented for Rmb10 a night.

The hotel has a Chinese restaurant, bar, shop and foreign exchange counter. The whole complex is badly maintained and has little character. The service and food are bad. A pleasantly-situated café beside the beach offers a small variety of soft drinks and beer and closes early in the evening. Despite its faults, the tourist centre is the most popular place to stay in Sanya because of its location on the very pleasant Dadonghai beach.

Tianyahaijiao, southernmost Hainan

Luhuitou Guesthouse
Luhuitou
tel. 877, 786

鹿回头宾馆
鹿回头

Double rooms with airconditioning Rmb80, with fan Rmb20

This group of 16 pleasant guesthouses, in a garden setting near the sea, was inspired by Liu Shaoqi when he visited Hainan soon after 1949, to be used as a retreat by high-ranking officials. Now it is open to overseas Chinese and foreign visitors. There are 146 rooms

within the complex, and three restaurants. The seashore here is not good for swimming. Luhuitou is about ten minutes by Hainan rocket from Dadonghai beach (Rmb4).

Xinya Hotel
Xinjian Lu
Tel. 952
cable 0068

新亚酒店
新建路

Double rooms Rmb60

This new 40-room hotel in the centre of Sanya offers reasonable accommodation, a good restaurant serving local specialities such as Hainan chicken, and a bar. It can arrange bus tickets, as well as boats to Hong Kong.

Sanya Hotel
Jiefang Lu
tel. 703

三亚宾馆
解放路

Double rooms with airconditioning Rmb36, without airconditioning Rmb20

Situated in the centre of town, this older building offers cheap accommodation.

Qiongnan Hotel

琼南宾馆

CTS will shortly open this modern hotel with comfortable rooms and Western and Chinese restaurants. It is situated in two blocks on the river front in Sanya.

Side-trips from Sanya

Beaches
Long beaches with fine sand and clear water are the main attraction of Sanya. The **Dadonghai** (Great East Sea) beach is the most developed. It is about four kilometres (2.5 miles) from Sanya and can be reached from the town by Hainan rocket (Rmb4). Street stalls on the road outside the beach sell fresh coconuts, pineapple and drinks.

About 24 kilometres (15 miles) west of Sanya is **Tianyahaijiao**, which literally means 'the limit of heaven and margin of the sea' though is more popularly known in English as the 'end of the earth'. The beach is marked by gigantic rocks engraved with Chinese characters and was a place to which disfavoured officials were exiled in ancient China. The most famous inscription are the two characters 'Tian Ya' (Heaven's Limit).

The beach has been developed as a popular tourist site, with souvenir shops and camels and ponies waiting for you to pose with them. A restaurant is being built above the beach. Minibuses run from Sanya and the Dadonghai Tourist Centre to the beach.

The most beautiful beach is **Yalong Bay**, about 25 kilometres (15.5 miles) east of Sanya. Except for a few fishermen's huts, fishing boats and one simple restaurant, this long beach is deserted and unspoilt. It is here that the government plans to develop tourism most extensively and already the foundations are being laid for the first of what is likely to be a series of joint-venture hotels and villa resorts. At present there is no public transport to the beach, which can only be reached by hired minibus or taxi.

Luhuitou

The rocky ridge above Sanya, called Luhuitou, which literally means 'deer turning its head', was given its name from a local legend. A young man from the Li minority tracked a deer with his bow and arrow from Wuzhishan to the southern bay below the ridge. On finding itself trapped the deer looked back and immediately turned into a beautiful Li woman who smiled at the man. The two later married and lived happily ever after.

But today Luhuitou is more famous among Western travellers for the Kangaroo Club, situated outside the gates of the Luhuitou Guest-house near the waterfront. Here a young man from Guangxi Province runs a superb restaurant which serves everything from pancakes in the morning, to giant garlic prawns at midnight. A group of Australians gave the restaurant its present name and erected suitable sign boards.

The nearby Luhuitou Restaurant has been set up in competition and offers similar dishes.

Eastern and Western Hawksbill Islands

These islands are notable for their coral villages. Buildings are made of coral, which can also be seen drying in the streets, on walls and along the beaches. Sampans to the island can be hired at the port. Hard bargaining may be necessary to fix a reasonable price.

Hui Village, Yanglan District

Hainan's smallest minority group, the Moslem or Huis, live in two villages on the western outskirts of Sanya. Arabic script can be seen on the buildings and there is a small mosque combining Hainan and Middle-eastern styles. Girls cannot marry outside the 5,000-strong community, unless their husbands convert to Islam.

Yacheng Village

Yacheng Village, 40 kilometres (25 miles) west of Sanya, is the site of the ancient prefecture of Yazhou. A gate tower and Confucius Temple can be seen. Here also are China's last two steles carved with the character shou (long life) in the handwriting of the Empress Dowager Cixi.

Central Route from Sanya to Haikou

The main attractions of this route are beautiful mountain scenery and Hainan's minoritiy nationalities who live in the upland area north of Sanya — the Li and Miao. There are minibuses and buses (Rmb4) running between Sanya and Tongshi, the capital of the Li and Miao Autonomous Prefecture, and a convenient place to break the journey. Several local buses a day run between Tongshi and Haikou (Rmb7).

Baoting

Baoting is a mountain town north of Sanya. Just northwest of Baoting is **Maoan**, a small town where most of Hainan's Miao people live. The Miao are a minority group dispersed broadly over southern China and several countries of Southeast Asia. In Maoan you can see villagers wearing their traditional national costume and buy hand-embroidered crafts.

Tongshi

Tongshi lies 87 kilometres (54 miles) north of Sanya and about two and a half hours away by bus. With its many new buildings, department stores and large free markets, it is the most important city on the central route across Hainan.

A short walk from the Tongshi Resort Hotel is the Li minority village **Fanmao**. The Li do not normally wear their national costume but will do so for group tours if given notice beforehand. Costumes aside, the village itself is interesting and the walk through the paddy fields lined with coconut palms offers a good opportunity to see rural Hainan.

There are two buses a day to Haikou, the first leaving at 7.30 am. Tickets can be bought at booths near the Wuzhi Mountain Guesthouse and at the bus station. There are frequent minibuses to Sanya which depart from the bridge in the town centre but can also be caught from outside the Wuzhi Mountain Guesthouse.

Hotels in Tongshi

Tongshi Holiday Resort

通什渡假中心

Double room Rmb75

Situated in the hills outside Tongshi, this attractive small hotel can be booked through the Haikou Tower Hotel, or in Hong Kong, tel. 3-659003.

Tongshi Villa
tel. 223565, 223560

通什旅游山庄

Double rooms with airconditioning and bathrooms, Rmb60

This 110-room modern hotel is pleasantly situated on the outskirts of town. It has a good Chinese restaurant, a coffee shop, bar and disco.

Wuzhi Mountain Guesthouse
Tongshi Lu
tel. 222981

五指山宾馆

Double room with airconditioning Rmb56, without airconditioning Rmb20

The 128-room hotel in the centre of town has been greatly improved by the recent opening of a new building. Within the hotel complex is the Shanchang Restaurant. Drinks are served on the roof-top. There is also a disco.

Tongshi Tourist Guesthouse
Haigan Lu
tel. 222688

通什旅游宾馆
海杆路

Double rooms Rmb60

This new hotel is adjacent to the tourist bureau. There is a bar and restaurant.

Tropical vegetation flourishes in Hainan's balmy climate

Qiongzhong County

The most famous sight in the county of Qiongzhong is **Wuzhishan**, the 'five-fingers mountain'. Wuzhishan is known for its fine timber, its flowers, gibbons and spotted deer which inhabit the slopes. The mountain is usually shrouded in mist and cloud. Even the locals seldom have the chance of seeing all 'five fingers'.

At the foot of the mountain the Taiping Scenic Region, three kilometres (two miles) from Tongshi, has been opened to tourists. There is a large waterfall in the region. To climb the mountain, start from Maoyang, a few kilometres north of Tongshi, passing the Giant Rock Bridge.

North of the county town can be found the largest deer breeding farm in Guangdong and Hainan, the **Guangdong Provincial Deer Farm**, home for some rare thamin, or Eld, deer.

Western Route from Haikou to Sanya

Along the western route can be found the **Songtao Reservoir**. Covering more than 100 square kilometres (38 square miles), this reservoir has become known as the Heavenly Pond since construction was completed in 1969. A wide range of fishing methods can be seen on the lake.

The chief place of interest in **Baodao Village** is the **Tropical Botanical Garden of Southern China**, which contains a wide range of tropical cash crops and rare plants. There is a guesthouse in the village.

On the west coast, near the town of **Zhonghe**, site of the old city of Danzhou, is the recently-renovated **Dongpo College**. The famous man of letters, Su Dongpo (1036–1101), lived here for three years from 1097. The academy was built during the second year of his stay. There is a well dug by him.

In the remote counties of Baisha, Changjiang and Dongfang in the mountainous areas along the coast, there are many minority nationality villages. On the third day of the third lunar month the Li people celebrate the Mountain Loving Festival. The best place to see the festival is at Xiaodongfang. Not far from here is the **Datian Thamin Protective Zone**, where the rare Eld deer are to be found.

Further south in **Ledong County** is the **Mount Jianfeng Natural Protective Zone**, a tropical forest with a great many species of animals and plants.

Zhanjiang

The rapidly developing city of Zhanjiang is the largest port and economic centre of southwestern Guangdong. It lies on the east shore of the Leizhou Peninsula, 492 kilometres (308 miles) from Canton. The city and surrounding regions were ceded to France in 1898 for 99 years but returned to China in 1949.

The region has become a primary economic base of offshore oil exploration in southern China and today is of more interest to the businessman than the tourist. Unless you are travelling to Hainan from Canton by bus and want to break your journey along the way, there is little in Zhanjiang itself to attract tourists. It is worth wandering through **Xiashan**, however, which is the old French settlement area behind the Haibin Hotel, where many faded old European-style buildings stand in wide avenues. The old French church has been renovated.

Since the Tang Dynasty immigrants have came from Putian in Fujian Province to the Leizhou Peninsula, accounting for the similarity between the Leizhou and Fujian dialects.

Getting to Zhanjiang

Zhanjiang is linked by daily CAAC flights to and from Canton. There are train connections from Guilin, Nanning or Liuzhou and the port can be reached by ocean-going ferries from Haikou, Canton and Hong Kong. Boats leave Tai Kok Tsui pier, Hong Kong, every other day at 7.30 pm. The journey takes 12 hours. Airconditioned buses leave the long distance bus station opposite the railway station in Canton at 7.30 pm (Rmb29.50). The journey takes 12 hours. There are several non-airconditioned buses from Hai'an. The journey takes four hours and costs Rmb7.

Hotels in Zhanjiang

Haibin Guesthouse
Haibin Lu, Xiashan
tel. 23555

海滨宾馆
霞山海滨路

Double rooms Rmb100, suites Rmb295

This former joint-venture hotel set in beautiful tropical gardens on the waterfront in Xiashan is now locally managed. There are 228 guestrooms in ten buildings, Chinese and Western restaurants, a bar, billiard room, video game room, tennis court, swimming pool, squash court, gymnasium and sauna. The food cannot be highly rated.

Airconditioned buses leave from the hotel to Canton in the early morning and evening (Rmb28). The hotel also operates a taxi service. Cheaper rooms are also available for Rmb45, though these are badly maintained.

Universal Hotel (Huanqiu Dajiudian)
Xiachi Liu Lu
tel. 39788
cable 1565

湛江环球大酒店
霞赤六路

Double rooms Rmb90

This new hotel in the centre of the city has two Chinese restaurants, a Western restaurant and a shopping arcade.

Zhanjiang Guesthouse
Yuejin Lu
tel. 37188

湛江宾馆
跃进路

Double rooms with airconditioning Rmb68, without airconditioning Rmb20

Standard and cheaper accommodation is offered by this hotel.

Side-trips from Zhanjiang

Huguangyan

This extinct volcano is situated about 20 kilometres (12.5 miles) southwest of Zhanjiang. It was named Huguangyan (Cliff of Lake Glitter) by an 11th-century prime minister because of the crater lake's crystal reflections. The lake, Jinghu, is situated in pleasant scenery. Several old temples can be found along its banks. The best known of these is Lengyan Temple, founded by a Song-Dynasty monk.

There are boats for hire and swimming facilities here. A taxi to the lake will cost about Rmb50. There are also local buses.

Fishing Villages

There are a number of fishing villages along the rugged coastline of the Leizhou Peninsula which, if you enjoy the sight of junks under sail and the life of a fishing community, are worth visiting. These include Dianbai, Wuchuan, Wailuo (in Xuwen County) and Liusha. These villages have hardly ever been visited by foreigners so expect to be greeted by surprise.

Meixian

Anyone from Meixian, the main city of northeast Guangdong Province, will tell you that its people are famous for their 'three abundances': soccer players, overseas compatriots, and the quality of their education. Possibly more relevant to foreign visitors is the fact that it is also an attractive city, with the feel of a medieval Italian town, set in an idyllic landscape.

Meixian people have a relaxed cosmopolitan air to them, no doubt nurtured by a history of foreign missionaries and traders, and now by a world of overseas Chinese. The land is rich in coal, and a major coalmine employing over 10,000 miners is only 50 kilometres away at Xingning, where the airport is. The potential for business and industry is great.

Meixian has developed three new towns in recent years. Neat, efficient-looking and characterless, these new residential extensions of the city came about largely through the support of overseas Chinese. Meixian has 710,000 inhabitants while its overseas compatriot population is 600,000 strong, half of them living in Indonesia.

As a city, Meixian's real charm lies in its elegantly laid-out old town on the bank of the Meijiang River. The harmonious two-storeyed facades could easily be placed in an old Italian city. The streets are relatively free of traffic and an evening stroll in this quarter is a good way to appreciate the gentle charm of Meixian life.

Northeast Guangdong Province, centering around Meixian, is the home of the Kejia (popularly transliterated as Hakka) people. They claim a separate ancestry to immigrants from the Yellow River Basin; and the Hakka dialect is distinct from both Cantonese and the dialect of Shantou. Linguists have established a close tie between the Hakka dialect and tenth-century speech. Overseas Hakkas are said to be one of the best educated groups of overseas Chinese.

The Hakka do not need to be reminded that they are different, for the name 'Hakka' means 'guests'. They were the last of the migrants who came south to live in this area. The first major southern migration of the Hakkas was in the ninth century when they settled mostly in Jiangxi Province. The next wave of migration, in the wake of invading Mongolians in the 12th century, brought them to Guangdong Province, where Cantonese and people of the Shantou region had already made themselves comfortable for several centuries. As distant cousins who arrived late, the Hakka were treated as outsiders, or guests, which inadvertently fortified their group identity. Today the Hakka number four million, concentrated in about 50 districts scattered widely over Guangdong, Jiangxi and Fujian Provinces. In spite of their dispersal, the Hakka are surprisingly consistent in their dialect and customs, and Meixian is considered the home of pure Hakka culture.

Visitors may get the chance to hear one traditional art in the Meixian Cultural Park — Hakka hill-singing. This is an old form of folk oral literature; all its lyrics are improvised and, within fixed limits, singers hold a musical discourse among themselves. The themes of Hakka hill-songs are predominantly love and courtship, but most of the singers at the park are quite elderly. Authorities have started to encourage this important folk custom, and since 1983 annual singing contests are held during the Mid-autumn Festival.

Getting to and around Meixian

By Air There are daily flights from Canton to Xinxing (Rmb80 one way), which is 54 kilometres (39 miles) from Meixian, leaving at 8.15 am. From the airport it takes about one and a half hours to get to Meixian. Buses wait for the plane to arrive. A new airport is due to open at Meixian at the end of 1987, with flights to and from Hong Kong and Shantou. CAAC's office is in the Overseas Chinese Mansion, tel. 22297.

By Bus There is a daily bus service connecting Meixian and Hong Kong. The journey is 640 kilometres (400 miles) and takes 14 hours. The usual route to Meixian is via Chaozhou and Shantou. The daily bus leaves Chaozhou's West Depot at 6.30 am, to arrive at noon (Rmb7).

An interesting way to return to Hong Kong is to proceed north to Xiamen (formerly called Amoy) in Fujian Province and board a Hong Kong-bound ferry there. From Meixian one can catch a daily bus going to Longyan in Fujian; the ride takes six hours. From Longyan one can either take a train or bus to Xiamen, the major port on the China coast south of Shanghai.

If you are heading to the northwest of Guangdong, there is a non-airconditioned bus to Shaoguan 400 kilometres (250 miles) away. The journey takes 12 hours.

Non-airconditioned buses to Meixian leave from the long distance bus station opposite the railway station in Canton at 6.30 pm. The journey takes 12 hours, and costs Rmb13.70.

By Boat An interesting, but tiring, journey is to take a ferry from Chaozhou to Songkou. The ferry goes upstream against the current and takes around 22 hours, leaving at 9.30 am and arriving around 8 am the next day. One needs to spend the night at Songkou and take the next morning's ferry to Meixian. This latter ferry runs on alternate days; it leaves at 6.30 am and arrives in Meixian 9.30 am. But the

journey is more enjoyable from Songkou to Chaozhou, which only takes about eight hours (see page 137). Tickets may be bought at the ferry piers in Chaozhou and Songkou; it is not necessary to book in advance.

   Transport in Meixian The staff at CTS in the Overseas Chinese Mansion, and at the adjacent Travel Bureau, are very helpful, though they do not speak English. One can hire a car from CTS to go into the country. The rate is Rmb0.9 per kilometre. The best way to get around the city of Meixian is to take a trishaw.

Hotels in Meixian

Overseas Chinese Mansion (Huaqiao Dasha)
Dongshan Dalu
tel. 22297

华侨大厦
东山大路

Double rooms with airconditioning Rmb35

Nicely located on the bank of the Mei River in the old town, this hotel commands a good view of the river and bridge. CTS is located at the front desk. There is a hotel shop.

Wuzhoucheng Hotel
(near the bus terminal)
tel. 23379

五洲城酒店
汽车站旁

Double rooms with airconditioning Rmb35

This hotel, opened in 1980, is situated near a new town complex. The bus to Hong Kong leaves from here.

Jiangnan Mansion
Jiangnan Dadao
tel. 23539

江南大厦
江南大道

Double rooms with airconditioning Rmb33; without airconditioning Rmb21; Dormitory Rmb4.50

This building, in the new section of the town, was converted into a hotel in 1983. Top-price rooms have TV and airconditioning.

Restaurants in Meixian

Hakka cuisine is famous for its salt-baked chicken. Other specialities include beancurd stuffed with meat. Its cooking is generally heavier than that of Shantou and Chaozhou, although both have similar dishes. Favourite local snacks include the refreshing grass jelly, a drink made from the flowers of *Mesona cinensis*, which can be tried at street stalls.

Wuzhoucheng Hotel Restaurant
tel. 23379

五洲城酒店飱室

This is the smartest restaurant in Meixian and serves high quality local food.

Jiaying Restaurant
Minzhu Lu
tel. 22258

嘉应酒楼
民主路

Open 10 am−8 pm, this restaurant is located in the old district. Its baked chicken is well known, and mushroom braised duck and Hakka stuffed beancurd are both worth a try. After 8 pm the restaurant is converted into a dance hall.

Overseas Chinese Hotel Restaurant (Huaqiao Dasha)
Dongshan Dalu
tel. 72297

华侨大厦
东山大路

Food here is of a high quality. One should try stuffed beancurd, salt-baked chicken, fish balls and meat balls.

Number One Restaurant (Diyi Fandian)
31 Dongmen Lu

第一饭店
东门路31号

An old restaurant with simple but good cooking. The restaurant has a large pastry corner selling traditional cakes.

Quansheng Mingyuan Café

泉声茗苑
百花洲戏院旁

This café, next to the mausoleum-like Baihuazhou Cinema, is the hottest nightspot in town. From 7.30 pm−10 pm live band music, snacks and cold beer are available — a good place for nostalgic music and clean family fun.

Sights in Meixian

Hakka Houses

If you do not get the chance to see a Hakka household in the countryside, this example in the centre of the new town, next to Baihuazhou Cinema, will give you a good idea of the extraordinary buildings arranged in a horseshoe shape, that house large extended

Italian-style villa in the heart of Meixian's old town

Trishaw operator, Meixian

families. At the front of the complex there are three doors beneath each of the three eaves. The larger central door leads into the ancestral hall. Behind this is a courtyard and then family quarters shaped into a semicircle. There is usually a pond, where carp and duck are raised, at the front.

It is well worth trying to visit a complete example in the countryside. Farmers are mostly very hospitable to strangers.

Ancestral Hall of Huang Zunxian

Near the new bridge is the home of the 19th-century intellectual, writer and ambassador, Huang Zunxian. The house, a good example of a traditional Meixian town house, is now kept open by his great grandson. In a balcony-study one can see a collection of Huang's writings and books.

More examples of Hakka households can be found near this house.

Side-trips from Meixian

Lingguang Temple

About 45 kilometres (28 miles) east of Meixian this temple can be reached by hired car or local buses.

Lingguang Temple is the major temple in this region. It is hidden in the folds of the Yingna Range, beneath Five Finger Peak. The temple was established in memory of the Zen monk Can Kui after his death in 861. It was expanded first in the 15th century and again in the 17th. Since then it has been restored several times. In front of the temple stand two towering junipers, said to be planted by Can Kui himself. Visitors need to walk for half an hour through a quiet valley and past a village, to reach the temple. The walk alone is worth the effort of the trip.

Songkou

This small town on the Mei River has barely been visited by foreigners in recent years, although the crumbling European-style buildings on the river bank are reminders of the earlier presence of overseas traders and missionaries. The town is full of old-world charm and it is well worth spending a day here, particularly if you intend to take the ferry to Chaozhou. From the town it is easy to walk into the hilly countryside, where traditional Hakka farming households can be seen.

Walk through the main street running parallel to the river. Small shops in the old houses are fascinating to browse in before you reach the countryside. Here you can follow the riverbank, past a small Buddhist temple where the monk and his assistant will give you a warm welcome. After a further half an hour you can reach the 19th-century **Rose Pagoda** (Meiguiting) standing on a hill above the river. Beneath the pagoda is a temple dedicated to the god of wealth.

There are several local buses a day from Meixian. The 50-kilometre (31-mile) journey takes about two hours. If you want to spend the night in the town, there are two modest hotels worth trying. **Songkou Meidong Hotel** (Songkou Meidong Lushe), Jiaotong Lu, is a large old building with a pleasant location overlooking East Lake and a park. There is no restaurant. Double rooms without airconditioning, but with a balcony and bath, are Rmb15. A bed in a dormitory is Rmb4.

Another cheap place to stay is the **Taoyuan Hotel** (Taoyuan Binguan), also in Jiaotong Lu. Rooms here do not have bathrooms, but on the first floor there is an excellent restaurant which stays open until 11 pm.

Ferry-ride down the Han River

The local ferry down the Mei River and then the Han River from Songkou to Chaozhou is a relaxing way of spending a day. The journey is 143 kilometres (89 miles) and the ferry stops at 23 villages on the way. It is a local daily boat which hardly ever sees idle wanderers. It leaves at 6.30 am, or 7.30 am Beijing summer time, every morning (Rmb7). When the current is strong, usually during the rainy season from June to October, one arrives at Chaozhou between 5 and 6 pm. In the dry winter months the ferry may not arrive until midnight.

The ferry is designed like a train carriage with two tiers of mattressed *tatami* running its full length. It is very comfortable. Refreshments and lunch are available.

Most of the river traffic is transport barges carrying coal and ore, sometimes towed in a row by tug boats, sometimes rowed by long oars. Beyond the riverbanks is unspoilt mountainous countryside.

Shaoguan

Shaoguan city administers an area which includes 12 counties and 4.3 million people in the northern-most part of Guangdong Province. Bordering on Hunan Province, Guangxi Autonomous Region, and Jiangxi Province, this remote mountainous district, which is the home of some 70,000 Yao minority people, is one of the least developed and poorest parts of Guangdong. But for the tourist it is also one of the most beautiful and interesting areas to explore.

The Shaoguan area has recently been selected for development by Guangdong tourism authorities, but as yet few foreigners have visited the region. The travel bureau is promoting activities like river rafting and hunting, as well as more traditional sightseeing. The better-known sights include the limestone Danxia Mountain range, the most celebrated Buddhist temple in southern China, and some important archaeological sites. Fossil remains of Maba Man, who lived 100,000 years ago, have been found here.

Particularly interesting in the area is the colourful culture of the Yao people in Liannan and Linxian counties — a five-hour bus journey from Shaoguan city.

Getting to Shaoguan

By Air There is one flight a day, except Mondays, between Canton and Shaoguan.

By Rail Shaoguan is on the main line leading north from Canton to Shanghai and Beijing. There are trains from Canton throughout the day. The journey takes five hours and costs Rmb14.

CITS (HK) organizes four-and five-day tours from Hong Kong to Shaoguan.

Hotels in the Shaoguan Area

Green Lake Villa Hotel (Bihu Shanzhuang)
Shahu Lu
Shaoguan
tel. 5109

碧湖山庄
韶关沙湖路

Double rooms (low season) Rmb80, (peak season) Rmb100

This 128-room new lake-side hotel is pleasantly located outside the town, surrounded by woods and hills. There are four two-storey units with high-class rooms, Chinese and Western restaurants, a shop and dance hall. A swimming pool is being built.

CITS has its office here and can arrange tours from the hotel. There is an amusement park near the hotel.

Shaohua Hotel
162 Jiefang Lu
Shaoguan
tel. 3109

韶华饭店
韶关解放路162号

Double rooms Rmb90

This new 17-storey hotel with 150 rooms is run by CTS, which has its office on the fifth floor. The first and second floors house a department store, the third floor two Chinese restaurants. There is also a concert hall and disco.

Songshan Hotel
Songshan Lu
Shaoguan
tel. 4161

松山饭店
韶关松山路

Double rooms Rmb85

This 150-room joint-venture hotel with reasonable quality facilities is used by many Hong Kong Chinese tour groups.

Jinjiang Villa Guesthouse
Danxia Mountains

锦江村宾馆
丹霞山

Double rooms Rmb80

A series of newly opened villas with comfortable rooms are located beside the Jin River. There is a good Chinese restaurant.

Yicui Hotel
Danxia Mountains

溢翠宾馆
丹霞山

Double rooms with airconditioning Rmb30, without airconditioning Rmb20

Also beside the river, this smaller CTS-run hotel has more basic accommodation, a shop and Chinese restaurant. The CTS office is beside the hotel and buses to Shaoguan leave from near here.

Side-trips from Shaoguan City

Danxia Mountains

The pink sandstone cliffs of Danxia, 50 kilometres (31 miles) north of Shaoguan city, are spectacular at sunrise. From the Sun-Watching Pavilion, more than 1,000 steps up from the road, you can see the sun rise from behind the bizarre Old Man Peak. The two other main peaks

are Conch Peak, which has a Buddhist stupa on the top, and Pearl
Peak. About 400 steps up the mountain is the Buddhist Biechuan
Temple, which dates back more than 300 years. A number of monks
still live here. It is well worth stopping at the temple on the way up the
mountain to watch the pre-dawn prayers.

Airconditioned tourist buses bound for Danxia Mountain leave
from outside Shaoguan railway station throughout the day.

The Jin River (Jinjiang) flows below the mountains. Boat trips are
available, and cost Rmb4 a person. These usually stop at a village
where souvenir stones can be bought. Rowing boats can also be hired.

Nanhua Zen Temple (Nanhua Chan Si)

Twenty kilometres (12.5 miles) south of Shaoguan city in Caoxi is the
Nanhua Zen Temple which in the seventh century was under the
charge of the Sixth Patriarch of the Southern School of Zen Buddhism,
Huineng.

The illiterate Huineng achieved enlightenment from overhearing a
recitation of the Diamond Sutra, and later became the Sixth Patriarch.
The Southern Sect originated from the temple, propounding a doctrine
of sudden enlightenment.

The temple is seven buildings deep. The earliest architecture dates
from the sixth century. It possesses many historic sculptures and
examples of calligraphy, as well as important Buddhist relics, the most
famous being a lacquer image of the Sixth Patriarch, moulded from his
body.

Nanhua Temple is the centre of Buddhism in Guangdong Province and a full training programme of Zen Buddhism has recently been reinstated here. CITS and CTS organize transport to the temple, which can also be reached by public bus.

Lion Cave (Shizi Yan)

In 1958 the fossil remains of Maba Man, who lived 100,000 years ago, were found in this cave, 1.5 kilometres (1 mile) southwest of Maba town in Qiujiang County. Also discovered in the cave were fossils of giant pandas, elephants and rhinoceros. These discoveries have proved that in the middle and later periods of the Pleistocene Epoch, primitive men had lived in this area. They have also provided important materials for the research of human evolution.

In 1968 *Maba Neanthropus*, who lived 5,000 years ago, was discovered in the valley of Lion Hill. Some 2,000 pieces of cultural artifacts from this period were unearthed from 108 tombs, revealing that the area had close economic and cultural links with the Yangzi River valley. Scenes from prehistoric life have been reconstructed in the five-storey cave. There is also a museum where artifacts and fossils can be seen, though Maba Man has been removed to Beijing.

Lechang County

In the small town of Pingchi are a series of strange limestone rocks. Best known is **Golden Cock Hill**, shaped like a cockerel. Pingchi is located in the northern-most part of Shaoguan district, about three hours by train from the city. The **Golden Cock Guesthouse** offers basic but clean accommodation and has an excellent restaurant that will serve food at any time.

From here you can take a raft 67 kilometres (42 miles) down the Jin River to the town of Lechang. There are a number of rapids but the scenery is rather dull. At present the six-hour trip is too long. But there are plans to shorten it, with the journey being completed by bus. The trip costs Rmb 25 and can be arranged at the Golden Cock Guesthouse or through CTS or CITS in Shaoguan.

Ancient Buddha Cave (Gufo Yan)

This vast cave, five kilometres (three miles) from Lechang Town, was the site of an ancient Buddhist temple. The cave has three layers and some impressive stalactites and stalagmites. There are tourist buses to the cave every hour from the town, 56 kilometres (35 miles) from Shaoguan. Local buses run throughout the day between Shaoguan and Lechang. Entrance to the cave is Rmb2.

Lianxian and Liannan Counties

The county town of Lianxian, **Lianzhou**, is situated 200 kilometres (125 miles) west of Shaoguan. It is 14 kilometres (9 miles) from the Yao minority town of **Liannan**. Beyond a walk along the riverbanks, the towns themselves have few attractions for tourists, but they form a convenient base from which to explore the very interesting surrounding Yao minority area. The mountain scenery is amongst the most beautiful in Guangdong, with its terraced hills and limestone crags.

Tourism is only just being developed in these counties and as yet there are few facilities for visitors. But local guides and staff at CTS and the Lianzhou Hotel do their best to make sure that a stay here is worthwhile.

For centuries these counties have been regarded as the most backward in Guangdong. In the Tang Dynasty the poet Han Yu was banished here to administer the region. Through his poetry, he turned the area into a centre of disaffection against the dynasty. Lianxian had a brief moment of glory when it was made the administrative capital of Guangdong during the Guomindang (Kuomintang) years.

Getting to Lianxian

Non-airconditioned local buses leave from Canton for Lianzhou every even-numbered day of the month. There are three local buses a day from Shaoguan. The journey takes five hours and costs Rmb7.

Getting around Lianxian

Only the toughest of travellers will want to rely on public transport to explore the counties of Lianxian and Liannan. There are local buses to the surrounding towns and villages but the main attractions are generally well off the paved road. Few Yao villagers have seen foreigners before, and your reception will be warmer if you are accompanied by a guide.

The best way to enjoy the area is to join a tour organized by an enterprising young man from Lianxian, Kim Kwong Ho (the name in Mandarin is Jin Guanghe). Mr Kim picks groups up from Shenzhen and Canton. For groups of less than ten, the price is Rmb100 a person a day for transport. For groups of more than ten the price includes food and accommodation as well. If you write to him a month in advance, it is possible to join one of the larger groups. He can be contacted at the Lianzhou Hotel. Mr Kim has a close rapport with Yao

villagers, making it possible for visitors to be welcomed warmly and to take photographs freely. The tour is flexible and informal. For those prepared to rough it a little, it is probably the most interesting and adventurous tour in Guangdong.

CTS, at the Lianzhou Hotel, has an English-speaking guide and vehicles which can be hired for Rmb60 for half a day. The hotel provides food, accommodation and transport for Rmb120 a day.

Hotels in Lianxian

Lianzhou Hotel
Lianxian

连州宾馆
连县

Rooms with airconditioning Rmb40; without airconditioning Rmb20

This newly-opened seven-storey hotel offers comfortable accommodation and friendly service, though some of the rooms are already a little shabby. Its restaurant serves excellent wild game, including stewed civet cat. *Dim sum* is served in the mornings. CTS has its office here and minibuses can be hired. The hotel runs a disco at weekends and has a foreign exchange service. Buses to Canton leave from here.

Liannan Guesthouse (Liannan Binguan)
Liannan

连南宾馆
连南

Double rooms (with airconditioning) Rmb40

This clean and comfortable guesthouse has no restaurant but there are restaurants in the town, the best being the Jialiang Restaurant.

Sights in the Lianxian Area

Huiguang Pagoda

Built in 468, this pagoda in Lianxian is one of the oldest brick pagodas in China. It dominates the town's skyline but is in a state of disrepair.

Yanxi Pavilion

Also in Lianxian, this pavilion was built in 785, during the Tang Dynasty, and was one of the subjects that the famous Tang poet Han Yu chose for his poetry.

The Minor North River

The river flows through three minor gorges. Tour groups can hire boats for Rmb5 a person.

Yao Minority Villages

Liannan County is home for about 50,000 Yao people and is one of the poorest but most colourful counties in Guangdong Province. There are 12 Yao tribes, each living along the banks of 12 streams and distinguished by slight variations in their mainly blue costumes. Guides can take you to a number of villages.

The Underground Silver Stream

Twenty-eight kilometres (17.5 miles) from Lianzhou is this 1,500-metre (4,900-foot) stream which can be explored by boat. It is essential to go with a guide, both to find the entrance of the stream and to locate a boatman from the nearby village. The stream is beautifully located in the mountains. The caves it flows through have a wealth of stalactites and stalagmites, which the boatman lights with just a single paraffin lamp.

Tian Lake, Tanling

This lake, 50 kilometres (31 miles) from Lianzhou and at a height of 1,600 metres (5,250 feet), is surrounded by natural forest. CTS is keen to take tourists there, either for a day-trip or to camp overnight. As yet there are no facilities, so go well-stocked with food and drink.

Dadongshan Hot Spring

The spring, 38 kilometres (24 miles) northeast of Lianzhou, is to be developed into a tourist resort, with baths and a guesthouse. At present the water flows out of an ugly pipe, then into a stream where you can bathe. It is remotely situated in the mountains and can only be visited with a guide.

The Pai Yao Minority of Northern Guangdong

The Pai Yao people live in an isolated mountainous area in northwest Guangdong Province. They are a small sub-group of the Yao, one of China's national minorites. There are around one and a half million Yao altogether, scattered as far afield as the Autonomous Region of Guangxi, Guangdong, Yunnan, Thailand and, nowadays, the United States and France. There are only 60,000 Pai Yao, however, and they live in this one region of China. In Liannan Yao Autonomous County the Pai Yao make up 45.6% of the local population. The balance consists of Han Chinese with a few Zhong, Man and other national minorities.

Although the Yao were once despised by the Chinese for their lack of civilization, since 1949 the Chinese government has been proud of its policy of respect for the distinct identity of the minority peoples, their traditions and lifestyles. As a result most of the Pai Yao continue to live in the pine-covered mountains in remote villages. Here they grow dry rice, sweet potatoes and a variety of other vegetables, and raise sway-backed pigs, chickens and cows.

The inaccessibility of the mountain villages of the region is striking. Few can be reached by vehicular transport. You may have to pick your way across stepping stones, or clamber up steep mountain paths to get to a village.

The village houses are solid structures of baked earth bricks, built directly on the ground. Roofs are thatched. Inside there is a large high-ceilinged central room with several doors leading to other smaller rooms. Simple wooden furniture stands on the beaten earth floor. Cooking is done in a rudimentary kitchen, in a *wok* placed over a fire built on the ground. Rice, a mixture of meats, including some small animals found in the hills, vegetables and beancurd make up the Yao diet. Most Yao have the healthy, rosy complexions usually associated with hill peoples.

The Pai Yao speak their own language which is unrelated to the Cantonese of the dominant majority around them. Some, but by no means all, speak Cantonese as well, and schooling in the Yao language is permitted in the villages. However, prominently displayed notices in the local government offices politely make the request: 'comrades, please speak *putonghua!*'

Most Yao wear their own traditional clothes which are dark coloured cotton tunics and trousers with white sashes, brightly-coloured embroidered purses and head-dresses. Silver coloured neck ornaments, once made of real silver, but nowadays of aluminium, are common. Some enterprising locals have — since the advent of the free market system — started buying articles of Yao dress to sell to interested Chinese or foreign visitors. Hairstyles are distinctively Yao, and in general, both dress and hairstyle denote the marital status of the wearer.

The Yao get married when they are around 20 years old. Traditionally the young people choose their own partners, rather than being bound by parental wishes like their Chinese neighbours. But the wedding customs themselves have much in common with the Chinese. Weddings are formal, elaborate and expensive. Horoscopes are consulted to confirm suitability; gifts are exchanged; feasts given and rituals undertaken to ensure the smooth transfer of the bride from her father's house to the groom's family.

The Yao are not bound by China's 'one-child' policy and children of all ages are much in evidence in the villages, running barefoot here and there, staring at any outsiders. Families of three or four children are quite common, and typically three generations live together.

Like the Chinese the Yao worship their ancestors and also practise a religion akin to Daoism, in which they propitiate a host of minor gods and spirits. Yao priests are very important in maintaining harmony between the world of people and the world of the supernatural, since they have the ability to talk to both worlds. But curiously, the Yao claim that gods must be spoken to in Chinese because they never learnt the Yao language.

Shantou

This is the second most important city in Guangdong Province. It has a population of 730,000 and the city is the district capital of the Swatow region, now officially called Shantou District. It was named a Special Economic Zone at the end of 1981, and two industrial districts are being developed.

The earliest record of immigration settlement in the Shantou region was in the second century BC in Jieyang (inland from the city of Shantou). The cultural characteristics of the region were determined much later by southward migration in the fourth century, when reportedly one in six people in central China moved south to escape the Tartar invasions. The mark left by demoted officials from the Tang Dynasty was also indelible: for instance the poet-official Han Yu was so well loved that even mountains and rivers in Shantou adopted the surname Han.

The dialect and customs of the Shantou region are better associated with the neighbouring province of Fujian than with Guangdong. The Minnan dialect of the Shantou region takes Xiamen speech as its norm, while Chaozhou (Chiu Chow) speech is its major variant. Outside the mainland; most Chinese in Thailand and the Philippines speak the dialect, and 80 per cent of Taiwanese are native Minnan speakers.

Part of Shantou was first opened to Europeans in 1858, after the Treaty of Tientsin. The first foreigners to settle in the city were in the opium trade. Several trading firms established a base, among them the Scottish company Jardine Matheson and the British American Tobacco Co. By the early 20th century Shantou was one of China's seven major commercial centres.

The older district of the city still recalls its history of international commerce with its eclectic collection of European architecture. The potential of Shantou as an international trading port was again resurrected when part of the city was designated a Special Economic Zone. Two areas are earmarked for development: Longhu District northeast of the old city and Guangao District to the southeast. Preferential terms for foreign investors have led to a number of new, joint-venture projects in these areas.

Despite the Special Economic Zone, Shantou remains an attractive city, combining the utility of a new town with the mellow atmosphere of a waned commercial centre. Colourful street stalls and small shops are scattered throughout the city.

Getting to Shantou

By Boat The most leisurely way of getting to Shantou is to take the ferry from Hong Kong. Ferries are scheduled to leave from Tai Kok Tsui in Kowloon every other day at 4.30 pm arriving in Shantou at around 7 am the next morning. There are six classes of tickets, ranging from Rmb223 for a two-person cabin to Rmb34 for a dormitory bunk. Return ferries to Hong Kong also leave on alternate days.

By Air There are three flights a week from Hong Kong, on Tuesdays, Thursdays and Saturdays (Rmb240). There are daily flights to Shantou from Canton at least once a day (Rmb101) and flights every Friday to Beijing (Rmb559) and to Kunming every Wednesday.

By Road Daily airconditioned buses connect Shantou with Shenzhen (eight hours, Rmb26), Canton (ten hours, Rmb28) and Fuzhou (12 hours, Rmb37). Several buses a day leave Shenzhen from the railway station between 6 and 7 am and 8 and 11 pm. Buses depart from the long-distance bus station in Canton at 7.50 pm.

In Shantou, buses to Shenzhen, Canton and Fuzhou leave in the mornings and evenings from outside Xinxing Guesthouse and the Overseas Chinese Hotel and pick up passengers throughout the town.

There is a frequent minibus service between Shantou and Chaozhou. Minibuses depart from near the Overseas Chinese Mansion in Chaozhou (Rmb 4), and at the square by the CTS City Branch in Shantou. Passengers are also picked up from the major hotels. The journey takes one hour.

Getting around Shantou

CITS, at the Shantou Peninsula Hotel (tel. 35226), is well organized and can arrange local tours for foreign tour groups, complete with guides who speak English, Japanese or Thai. Accommodation and forward travel arrangements can also be arranged by CITS.

CTS, who mainly handles overseas Chinese visitors, is located in the Overseas Chinese Mansion. It also arranges tours and transportation but has no English-speaking guides.

Transport in Shantou is provided by minibuses, which run from near the vehicle ferry, along Waima Lu to the Overseas Chinese Hotel and the Longhu Hotel (Rmb1). There are also motorized and pedal trishaws.

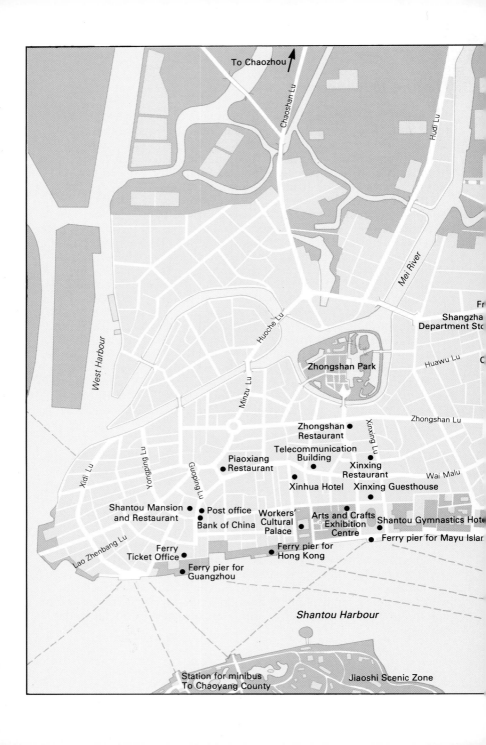

To Chaozhou

Chaoshan Lu

Hudi Lu

Mei River

West Harbour

Huoche Lu

Minzu Lu

Fr
Shangzha
Department Sto

Zhongshan Park

Huawu Lu

C

Zhongshan Lu

Xidi Lu

Yongping Lu

Guoping Lu

Zhongshan
Restaurant

Telecommunication
Building

Xinxing Lu

Xinxing
Restaurant

Wai Malu

Piaoxiang
Restaurant

Xinhua Hotel

Xinxing Guesthouse

Shantou Mansion
and Restaurant

Post office

Bank of China

Workers'
Cultural
Palace

Arts and Crafts
Exhibition
Centre

Shantou Gymnastics Hote

Ferry pier for Mayu Islar

Lao Zhenbang Lu

Ferry
Ticket Office

Ferry pier for
Hong Kong

Ferry pier for
Guangzhou

Shantou Harbour

Station for minibus
To Chaoyang County

Jiaoshi Scenic Zone

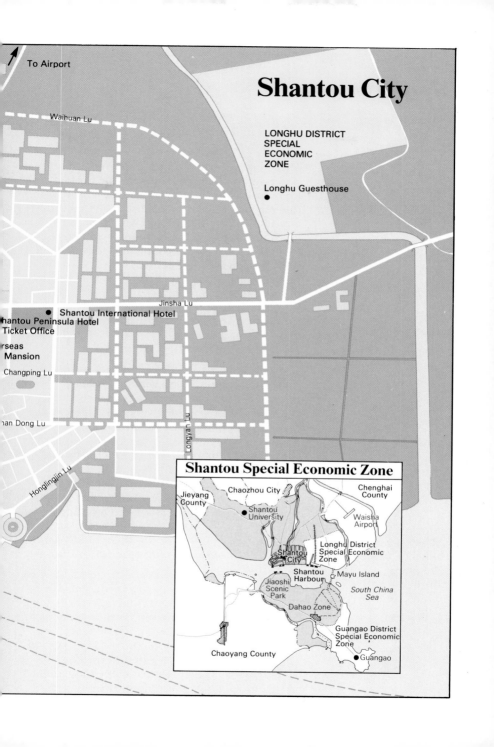

Hotels in Shantou

Shantou International Hotel
Jinsha Lu
tel. 51212
tlx. 45475
fax. 52250

汕头国际大酒店
金沙路

Rooms US$40 (US$43 October–December); suites from US$215 (US$220 October–December)

This 26-storey joint-venture international standard hotel located the near the Special Economic Zone is due to open early in 1988. It is managed by Hong Kong-based Lee Gardens International, and will be Shantou's top hotel. It has seven food and beverage outlets, a range of shops, billiard room, and a fully-fledged business centre, with fax, word processor, interpretation services, and a multi-purpose function room.

Chauffeur-driven limousines are available for tranfers to the ferry or airport.

Longhu Guesthouse
Special Economic Zone
tel. 60578
tlx. 45458
cable 2160

龙湖宾馆
金沙路

Double rooms Rmb85, 128; suites Rmb140, 224

This joint-venture hotel with 237 rooms, opened in 1984 and recently completed with the addition of a second wing, has all the facilities of an international hotel, including Chinese restaurant, coffee shop, bar, fast food shop, disco, function room, shopping arcade, business, health and entertainment centre, travel desk and taxi service. Its Pearl Restaurant serves good Cantonese and Chiu Chow dishes, as well as *dim sum* in the mornings.

Shantou Peninsula Hotel (Tuodao Binguan)
Jinsha Dong Lu
tel. 35226

鮀岛宾馆
金沙东路

260 rooms. Double rooms with airconditioning Rmb78; without airconditioning Rmb33; suites Rmb136

This 260-room, 13-storey modern hotel also designed for businessmen coming to the Special Economic Zone is near the Overseas Chinese Mansion. It has a good banquet restaurant (Jinfenglou), a coffee shop, bar and small shop. CITS has its office here. The Jinfenglou is particularly recommended as an excellent venue to entertain business guests.

Overseas Chinese Mansion (Huaqiao Dasha)
Shanzhang Lu
tel. 33966
cable 3333

华侨大厦
汕樟路

Double rooms with airconditioning Rmb44, 50; without airconditioning Rmb26; dormitory beds Rmb7

This large hotel, managed by CTS, has some 400 rooms in two blocks. Most overseas Chinese tour groups stay here. All rooms in the 15-story East Building are airconditioned. The South Building has cheaper unair-conditioned rooms and dormitory beds. There are restaurants, shops, a snack bar, travel and foreign exchange facilities and a taxi service.

Shantou Gymnastics Hotel (Shantou Tiyu Binguan)
Haibin Lu
tel. 76466

汕头体育宾馆
海滨路

Double rooms Rmb75

This joint-venture hotel which opened in 1987 overlooks the waterfront and sports ground in the old town. It has 45 comfortable aircon-ditioned rooms with bathroom, refrigerator, telephone and TV. There is a coffee shop, restaurant, dance hall and shop.

Xinxing Guesthouse
1 Xinxing Lu
tel. 72871, 71041

新兴宾馆
新兴路 1 号

Double rooms Rmb42 with airconditioning; without airconditioning Rmb21

This old-fashioned hotel is convenienty located near the waterfront in the old town. Most of the rooms in the new wing are airconditioned. Bus tickets to Shenzhen and Canton can be bought at the hotel.

Xinhua Hotel
Wai Malu
tel. 76202

新华饭店
外马路

Double rooms with airconditioning Rmb30

This new hotel is also located in the centre of the old city. All rooms have TV and telephone. It has a restaurant and a teashop.

Mayu Island Hotel
tel. 72220

妈屿宾馆

Double rooms without airconditioning Rmb36

Situated above the beach on the small island of Mayu at the mouth of Shantou harbour, this hotel is on the site of the former residence of the British customs officer, which now constitutes one wing of the hotel. It has about 20 rooms and is popular with domestic and

overseas Chinese. Advance booking should be made in the summer. There is a restaurant serving good seafood, and disco.

Restaurants in Shantou

One of the pleasures of a stay in Shantou is the excellent Shantou (Swatow) or Chaozhou (Chiu Chow) cuisine, known for its subtle flavours. Specialities are seafood, such as fried shrimp and crabmeat balls, and rice noodles. Shantou is also famous for its strong Oolong tea, served in tiny cups wherever you go.

Food is rarely disappointing in Shantou and Chaozhou, with street food often as good as that offered in restaurants and available late into the night. On Mayu Island there are numerous small, privately-owned snack shops on the beach which serve good rice noodles and seafood.

Xinxing Restaurant
77 Xinxing Lu
tel. 3281

新兴飱室
新兴路

This is the most famous restaurant in Shantou. One particularly popular dish is Old Xu's noodles (Lao Xu Chaoguo). Aside from the Shantou specialities of meat balls and rice noodles, one may also try their soyabean chicken, braised mushroom and duck's feet, and oyster omelette.

Chaozhou Restaurant
Changping Lu
(opposite Overseas
Chinese Mansion)

潮州菜馆
长平路

This 24-hour restaurant has received wide acclaim for its success as a private enterprise and has even been televised. The food is first class, the service good and the surroundings comfortable. Oyster omelette, braised squid and grilled prawns, as well as rice noodles, are just some of the specialities it has to offer. It will also prepare special dishes, such as game birds and sea turtle, if orders are placed a day in advance. This is one of Shantou's more expensive restaurants. Expect to pay at least Rmb20 a head.

Xinqiang Restaurant
Changping Lu

信强飱厅
长平路

Across the street is another privately-owned restaurant. The food here matches the Chaozhou Restaurant and is about half the price. The service is friendly but the surroundings more basic — though improvements are due to begin soon.

Piaoxiang Snack Restaurant
50 Tongping Lu

飘香小吃店
同平路

This state-owned restaurant was originally the Xu Family Ancestral Hall. The restaurant is known for its rice noodles and dumplings. Other Shantou specialities are also good. The restaurant opens at 6.30 am for breakfast and closes at 11.30 pm.

Shantou Mansion
Yongping Lu

汕头大厦
永平路

This restaurant, now half a century old, is located in the heart of the old city. The surroundings may look as if they are about to crumble, but it serves high quality Shantou food. Specialities include *taijin* taro paste and steamed crab. There is an excellent bakery on the ground floor.

Sights of Shantou

Jiaoshi Scenic Park

Across the harbour from the city, Jiaoshi was the favourite residential district of foreign traders. Jardine Matheson, the long-established British trading company, used to have its residential quarters here. This hilly district with enormous boulders, woods and ponds makes an attractive natural park. It is known locally as 'the stone forest at the sea corner'. There is a restaurant on the peak and a teahouse near the rock caves. Ferries run all day between Jiaoshi and Shantou, and the crossing takes 15 minutes.

Blue Clouds Crag (Qingyunan)

This mountain to the east of Dahao township on the outskirts of the city has 18 caves.

Zhongshan Park

This huge park has a cinema, a theatre, a zoo, an exhibition hall and a lake on which rowing boats are rented out. It is particularly worth visiting early in the morning during the traditional Chinese workout.

Lao Zhenbang Lu and Wai Malu

There is a wealth of crumbling, European-style architecture in this district, particularly colourful in the evenings when it is packed with street stalls.

Arts and Crafts Exhibition Centre

The exhibition centre (open 7.30 am–6 pm) is a good place to find traditional Shantou and Chaozhou products, though the service is particularly surly. The Shantou area is famous for its drawn lace products and gold-painted wood carvings. Chaozhou musical instruments and exotic embroidery can also be purchased here. Shantou Lace Products Company, 49 Wai Malu, also sells lace and embroidery.

Mayu Island

The small fishing island at the mouth of Shantou harbour has now become a popular beach resort with local and overseas Chinese. A hotel and numerous cafés have been built.

There is a famous temple devoted to Tianhou, goddess of the sea, built in 1862, and a sister temple built in 1928. Tianhou is well known for her protection of fisherfolk, and Mayu used to be populated with chickens set free by worshippers who honoured the goddess. Here can be seen the inlaid porcelain, wood and stone carvings that are a particular feature of buildings in the Shantou and Chaozhou areas.

The village is full of traditional Shantou houses overlooking the harbour where junks under full sail can be seen. The beach itself has no such old-world atmosphere. It is usually packed with people swimming, playing ball and eating. This is a good place to wonder at the changes that have taken place in the lifestyle of the Chinese in the last ten years. The colour of the sea is usually chocolate brown.

Ferries to the island leave from the bottom of Xinxing Lu at 9.30 am and 3.30 pm, returning at 5.30 pm and 10.30 pm.

Side-trips from Shantou

Chaozhou (see page 161) and Chaoyang County are the two main scenic areas outside Shantou that can be covered in day-trips. CITS, and the Shantou Special Economic Zone Tourism Corporation based at the Longhu Hotel, organize special tours complete with English-speaking guides.

Chaoyang

Minibuses run all day between Shantou and Miancheng, the main town in Chaoyang County which lies south of the Liusha River. They leave from either side of the river near the Jiaoshi ferry. The trip takes about half an hour and costs Rmb4. From Miancheng, minibuses or motorbikes will take you to the sights. There are also two hotels in the town — an **Overseas Chinese Hotel** and the new **Dongshan Binguan**.

North Cliffs (Bei Yan) Situated on the East Hills beyond Chaoyang's East Gate, there are a series of stone caves fashioned into Daoist temple grottoes and monasteries.

West Cliffs (Xi Yan) Two kilometres (1.25 miles) west of Miancheng is the most famous temple of the district. The Zen master Wei Zhao initiated monk Da Dian here in 765. In the temple is a double male-female tree reputed to be over a thousand years old.

Haimen Beach and Lotus Rock (Lianhua Feng) About ten kilometres (six miles) out of Miancheng on the edge of the town of Haimen is a beach, famous for its large boulders. The largest is Lotus Rock (Lianhua Feng) which is split into five sections resembling a lotus flower. It has inscriptions relating to the last Song-Dynasty court. The beach here has soft sand and is good for swimming.

Overlooking the beach is the modest **Haimen Lotus Garden Hotel**, which has recently opened. Non-airconditioned double rooms, with bathroom, fan and TV, cost Rmb36 and Rmb42. There is a good restaurant, open noon−2 pm and 5−7 pm.

Lingshan Temple (Lingshansi) Twenty kilometres (12 miles) from Miancheng is the major temple of the Shantou region. It was first built by the Zen monk Da Dian in 791, and although the temple has been rebuilt several times over the centuries, it is still rich in cultural artifacts. Behind it is a bell-shaped pagoda, known as Gujingta, or Old Mirror Pagoda, where Da Dian is believed to have had his Nirvana. Outside is a pavilion where Han Yu, a Tang-Dynasty man of letters, left his clothing to the abbot as a keepsake. Hence the name Liuyiting (the Pavilion where the Clothing was Left).

Chaozhou

The historic city of Chaozhou was first designated district capital of this part of China in 413. Many famous poets and scholars have worked here since the Tang Dynasty. Today the people of Chaozhou are known for the refinement of their music and opera, the quality of their crafts and the subtlety of their cuisine.

The city is attractively set on the Han River. Rolling hills stretch out from either bank; a 16th-century stone pagoda overlooks the city from the south, and West Lake Park, with its mountain of engraved boulders and lake, lies at the northeast corner of the city. Chaozhou has a colourful civility befitting an old city. Its narrow streets, which are entered through fortress gates, are bordered by crumbling but beautiful town houses and numerous stalls which make and sell fresh noodles. They would not be out of place in southern Italy.

Chaozhou can be visited as a day-trip from Shantou, an hour away, or if you are prepared to stay in less comfortable accommodation than can be found in Shantou, it can be used as a base from which to explore the surrounding area.

Getting to Chaozhou

By Road Chaozhou is best reached from Shantou. Buses and minibuses leave for Shantou frequently thoughout the day (Rmb4). Minibuses leave from the square at the end of Wai Malu but can be stopped anywhere along Wai Malu. They can also be caught from the Overseas Chinese Hotel.

The road was originally an old railway line which was dismantled by the Japanese during World War II. If one takes a taxi it is well worth side-tracking into a traditional Shantou village. Off the main road there is much evidence of the traditional Shantou art of masonry. Not only do villagers make pillars and beams out of granite, but even electric wire posts are granite poles.

Chaozhou can also be reached by road from Meixian. Two buses leave Meixian bus station at 6 am. The journey takes about six hours, and costs Rmb7. Minibuses also leave from the Overseas Chinese Mansion in Meixian.

There are direct buses between Canton and Chaozhou. They leave from the long distance bus station opposite the railway station at 8.40 am and 6.40 pm. The journey takes 12 hours and costs Rmb14.80. There are also airconditioned bus connections with Hong Kong, Canton, Shenzhen, Xiamen and Zhongshan. For outward journeys,

buses leave Chaozhou from outside the Overseas Chinese Mansion. Buses to Hong Kong can be booked at this hotel.

By Boat There is a ferry connection with Meixian, via Songkou. The scenic 143-kilometre (89-mile) journey on the Mei and Han Rivers to Chaozhou takes between 12–18 hours (see page 137).

Getting around Chaozhou

CTS and the Travel Bureau are located in the Overseas Chinese Mansion (tel. 732151); at present they have no staff who speak English.

One can take local buses to visit the surrounding countryside. Buses going out of town leave either from the east depot by the East Gate or from the main station at the west depot on Xi Malu. CTS can organize minibuses for groups. At present there are no taxis, though motor tricycles will be able to take you a short distance into the countryside.

Sights and places of interest between Chaozhou and Shantou are more easily visited from Shantou where cars can be hired from all the major hotels (about Rmb200 a day).

The ferry pier is a few hundred yards north of the East Gate. Tickets are on sale at the River Port Authority across the street (tel. 732415).

Hotels in Chaozhou

Overseas Chinese Mansion (Huaqiao Dasha)
Huancheng Xi Lu
tel. 732151

华侨大厦
环城西路

Double rooms with airconditioning Rmb37, 54; without airconditioning Rmb21

Opened in 1980, this is the largest tourist hotel in Chaozhou and can accommodate 300 guests. CTS and the Travel Bureau have their offices here. There is a good banquet restaurant (see below).

Chaozhou Mansion
Xihe Lu
tel. 732121

潮州大厦
西河路

Double rooms with airconditioning Rmb42; without airconditioning Rmb18

This 200-room hotel is convenient for business visitors. The ground floor is a shopping centre, the first floor used for business meetings. The hotel extends upwards from the second floor. The opening hours of its restaurant are the same as at the Overseas Chinese Mansion.

**Chaozhou Travel
Service Hotel**
Huancheng Xi Lu
tel 732171

潮州旅游服务社
环城西路

*Double room with airconditioning Rmb31;
without airconditioning Rmb19*

This hotel was renovated in 1980. A minibus
service to Shantou operates from here.

Restaurants in Chaozhou

Chaozhou is the home of the original cuisine of the Shantou region
known outside China as Chiu Chow food. Most restaurants and street
stalls offer good food, though the choice of restaurants and opening
hours are more restricted than at Shantou.

**Overseas Chinese
Mansion Restaurant**
Overseas Chinese
Mansion
tel.732151

华侨大厦飡室
华侨大厦

The restaurant can cater for a banquet of 400
guests, but it is usually quite empty. The chef
is well known in Chaozhou for his skill in
bringing out the lighter, natural flavours of the
ingredients in his cooking. Dishes such as eel
and preserved vegetable soup and steamed
mushroom and bamboo shoot soup are
delightful supplements to the famous Shantou
meatballs and seafoods. Opening hours are
restricted (7−8.30 am, 11 am−2 pm, 5−7.30
pm) except for banquets.

**Hurongquan
Restaurant**
140 Taiping Lu

胡荣泉飡室
太平路140号

This famous restaurant opened in 1909. The
old two-storey building is rather dilapidated
but the restaurant is popular with local
people. The fare is simple and substantial.
They serve a good spiced rice noodle and their
mushroom soup with bamboo shoots is also
delicious. If you cannot speak Chinese just go
down to the open kitchen on the street and
simply point. It is open 8 am-midnight.

Chaoan Restaurant
169 Taiping Lu

潮安饭店
太平路169号

A state-owned restaurant across the street
from Hurongquan, the food here is also plain
and substantial. The restaurant is in an old
mansion which was once a large fabrics shop.
It is open 8 am−10 pm.

168

West Lake Café
West Lake Park

西湖飱室
西湖公园

This small restaurant by the lake is open only 8 am – 5 pm. It has a charming atmosphere and its speciality is fish from the West Lake.

Sights of Chaozhou

Kaiyuan Temple

Near the East Gate, this Tang-Dynasty temple was built in 738 by imperial decree as one of ten major temples in China. It is the oldest in eastern Guangdong but is now only a third of its original size. Its architecture dates from the Tang to Qing Dynasties. Some of the stone carving was done during the eighth century, such as part of the four columns in the centre courtyard, symbolizing the four corners of the universe. The stone balustrades outside the Main Hall, dating from the Tang and Song Dynasties, have carvings on 18 sides. From a wooden scaffold hangs a bronze bell, cast in the Song Dynasty, which weighs 150 kilograms. The library tower keeps the Dazangjing, or the Collection of Buddhist Scriptures, totalling 7232 volumes, donated by Emperor Qianlong of the Qing Dynasty.

During the Cultural Revolution much of the temple was damaged and all the Buddhas destroyed. Now, thanks to money being donated from overseas Chinese, they are being restored. The high standard of work is evidence that Chaozhou's traditional craftsmanship is still thriving.

The temple has a solemn majesty distinct from most southern temples. Resident monks run a full religious service in the temple.

West Lake Park (Xihu Gongyuan)

This large park was first opened in the eighth century. There are various gardens dotted about the hill within the park and it is particularly famous for its 160 pieces of calligraphy engraved on boulders, some of them dating back to the eighth century. There are two temples at the western corner of the park. Here, inscribed on a boulder, is what is meant to be the most exquisite *xin* character, meaning heart. It was improved by three generations of the same family during the Ming Dynasty before it was finally carved.

The West Lake Café is a good restaurant for lunch. It serves fish caught in the lake.

Phoenix Pagoda (Fenghuangta)

This 16th-century stone pagoda on the river downstream from Xiangzi Bridge and south of Hanshan Mountain commands a view of the whole region from its summit. The location of the pagoda has been carefully selected for its good *feng shui* (geomantic influences) and guarantees the prosperity of the city.

Hanyu Temple

This small temple was built in the 12th century in memory of the Tang poet Han Yu (768–824) whose term of office in Chaozhou was crucial to the development of the region. The temple is modest and intimate and is sheltered by an ancient tree on the slopes of Bijia Hill. The area is being developed as a scenic spot, with another temple and several pagodas planned.

Xiangzi Bridge

This bridge in front of the impressive East Gate was constructed in the 12th century. The middle section of the bridge used to be a row of 18 vessels which formed a floating gate. The original reason for this design was to overcome the difficulty of building foundations in the strong mid-stream current. This was the first bridge in the world to have such a gate, but the Communist government converted it to a nondescript steel and concrete construction.

Zhuo Family Mansion (Zhuofu) and the Jinshan Embroidery Workshop (Jinshan Guxiuchang)

This mid 19th-century mansion in Zhongshan Lu is supposedly an important cultural monument under the protection of the municipal government, but it has been thoroughly vandalised and most of the estate is lost to neighbouring buildings. The embroidery factory has taken over the remainder of the mansion, which makes it a fascinating workshop to visit. The Gu-style embroidery of Chaozhou is a well-known craft; it is richly ornate and its embroidered figures are in low relief. Finished pieces are on sale here, including Chaozhou opera slippers and hats. Small pieces cost Rmb18 while the bride's head-dress costs Rmb60. Most of the work has been commissioned by overseas Chinese. The government embroidery factory, next to the west gate entrance to West Lake Park, can also be visited. It has some exquisite picture-size embroideries for sale.

Temple roof, Mayu Island, Shantou harbour

Street life, Shantou

Pointing the way, Shantou

Refreshments, near Chaozhou

Taiping Lu and Kaiyuan Lu

These two streets are in the heart of the old city and are full of small shops and street stalls. A walk along the streets and neighbouring alleys, with delapidated mansions on either side, is like stepping back to medieval times. The streets are at their best just before sunset.

Side-trips in Chaozhou County

East Mountain Lake (Dongshanhu)

This lake located at the foot of Sangpu Mountain mid-way between Shantou and Chaozhou is now being developed as a tourist resort. There are hot spring baths and masseurs. In a cave between the peaks of two mountains is **Ganlu Temple**, with a large statue of the Laughing Buddha, built in the Song Dynasty. Also near the lake is the tomb of Lin Daqin, the Ming-Dynasty scholar who died in 1531. There are a number of statues of horses before the tomb.

A hotel beside the lake is currently being extended but it is still possible to stay there.

Tomb of Wang Dabao

This tomb near the banks of the Han River about 20 kilometres (12.5 miles) northwest of Chaozhou has the best stone statues of animals in the region. Wang Dabao was a Song-Dynasty official.

House of Cong Xigong

This family house belonging to the Qing-Dynasty Overseas Chinese businessman Cong Xigong. It is noteworthy for its four intricate stone-carved plaques and is a fine example of a traditional Chaozhou house. It is located just off the Shantou Lu, about 30 kilometres (19 miles) from Chaozhou.

Zhongshan County and Zhuhai

For over four centuries Zhongshan's history has been shaped by overseas barbarians and overseas Chinese. So it is appropriate that today this county over the border from Macau acts as a corridor between east and west representing instant China for foreign tourists, and a window on the West for the Chinese.

Before 1557 the people of Heungshan, on the southwestern shore of the Pearl River estuary, lived in relatively prosperous obscurity. Their land was rich from river silt and their major town of Shekkei (now officially called Shiqi) was a busy inland port and market centre, but they lived far beyond the attention of Beijing. The imperial court paid scant notice when the Portuguese settled on a tiny peninsula in Heungshan which they named Macau, but the presence of overseas barbarians soon had its effects on the local people. Within a few years Macau became a booming entrepot for China's foreign trade with Japan and Europe. The merchants of Canton made their fortunes selling silk, porcelain and other luxurious goods in exchange for Japanese silver and spices from the Indies.

The merchants and mandarins (Portuguese word, meaning commander) of Heungshan also prospered. There is no evidence that Macau was ceded by treaty and it is most likely that the Portuguese came to an arrangement whereby they paid for Macau with rent and customs duty on its cargoes.

In addition, the neighbouring Chinese were able to sell food and building materials to the settlers, and, because the Portuguese refused to do manual work, farmers and artisans moved to Macau. One profound result was the first culinary interchange of East and West. The Portuguese introduced China to peanuts, sweet potatoes, lettuce, green beans, pineapples, papayas, shrimp paste and spices from India and Africa, as well as coffee and wine. In return they adopted Chinese rhubarb, celery, ginger, soy and tangerines (so named after their success for transplanting in Tangiers). The Chinese were the cooks in Macau and they taught the Europeans the benefits of fast frying food to seal in the flavour. And, most historically important, the Portuguese discovered the delights of drinking tea.

In other respects the Chinese helped change the life style of the Portuguese and later Europe by making available silks and other fine fabrics which were vastly superior to the coarse, heavy cloth worn in Europe. Western architecture was also affected by Chinese examples of high-ceilinged rooms and courtyards.

European ideas spread more slowly but their effect was to be far reaching. Some of the Chinese who worked in Macau were converted to Christianity, and others gained a knowledge of the world beyond China, which in traditional Chinese maps was reduced to a vague fringe around the Middle Kingdom.

With a window to the West in Macau, people from Heungshan became the first Chinese to migrate en masse to Western countries. The first groups are recorded leaving in 1820, and many more followed. Where they went and what they did is well illustrated in Shiqi's Sun Yatsen Memorial Hall today. Maps show Heungshan migrants settling in countries throughout the world, from South America to Scandinavia, South Africa to New Zealand.

Many migrants encountered horrendous conditions in gold mines, on the railways and in squalid Chinatowns. However, some prospered and returned home to build ostentatious tower-houses and mercantile companies. Just as importantly, young Chinese returned with Western ideals of democracy and found the feudal regime of the Manchus insupportable.

This opposition was spearheaded by Sun Yatsen, who left his home in Heungshan to organize a revolution, which toppled the Manchus in 1911. In his honour the county was renamed 'Chungshan' (Sun Yatsen was also known as Sun Chung-shan), now spelt 'Zhongshan'. The 20th century has seen more upheavals for the area. It suffered considerable casualties in World War II and during the 1949 revolution. Much worse was the Cultural Revolution, when all Chinese with overseas connections were considered subversive. Since just about everyone in Zhongshan has family abroad this was a dark time.

Today, in contrast, Zhongshan is enjoying a new era of prosperity and freedom, thanks to investments by its overseas Chinese and a burgeoning tourist industry. Zhongshan County supports a population of about 1.3 million in its 1780 square kilometres (687 square miles). It is still basically agricultural, with over 50 different crops. Rice is the major product, followed by sugarcane, vegetables and fruits such as lychees and mangoes. Throughout the countryside there are piggeries, duck farms and fish hatcheries, with fishing communities along the coast.

Increasingly there are modern industries, particularly in the Special Economic Zone of Zhuhai and in the principal town Shiqi. The major products are building materials, Western medicines, textiles, processed food, electronic components, glass and bicycle parts. A large number of the new factories, as well as new hospitals and apartment blocks, have been built with investments from overseas Chinese whose ancestral home is Zhongshan. These foreign cousins are now made very welcome as visitors, and a special government office helps track down families for those in search of their roots.

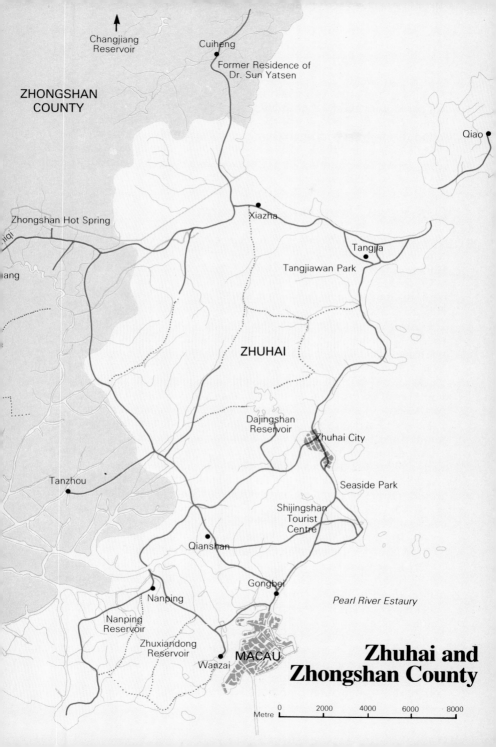

Zhongshan attracts many other visitors. Chinese from other parts of Guangdong and farther afield come to pay homage to Dr Sun, and then explore the holiday resorts of the area. Foreign visitors have found this to be the most convenient and satisfying experience of instant China, and the tour can be made on a one-day excursion from Hong Kong. The number of visitors to Zhongshan has steadily risen in the past few years, more and more staying overnight.

Getting to Zhongshan and Zhuhai

By Boat via Macau Almost all foreign visitors use one of the vessels which commute between Hong Kong and Macau to reach Zhongshan. Boeing Jetfoils (Far East Hydrofoil Co) make the 65-kilometre (45-mile) 55-minute trip every half hour between 7 am and 5 pm in winter, 6 pm in summer, plus frequent departures from 6.30 pm–1.30 am (US$8.50 first class, US$7.30 second class on weekdays; US$9.2 and US$8 weekends and public holidays; US$11.30 and US$10 night service). Bookings can be made through Ticketmate and wharf offices in Hong Kong. Jetcats (jet-propelled catamarans of Hongkong and Macao Hydrofoil Co) operate ten trips a day, taking 70 minutes (US$6 weekdays, US$7.50 weekends and holidays). Hydrofoils (Hongkong and Macau Hydrofoil Co) make 22 trips a day between 8 am and 5 or 6 pm, taking 75 minutes (US$6 weekdays, US$7.50 weekends and holidays). Ferries (Shun Tak Shipping) make six daily sailings, taking about three hours (US$4 for reclining seat, up to US$20 a cabin).

Modern, comfortable High Speed Ferries have five round-trips a day, making the journey in 100 minutes (US$4.50–7.00).

All of the above depart from the Macau wharf on Hong Kong island. Hover-ferries (Sealink Ferries Co) leave from Shamshuipo in Kowloon with eight trips a day, taking an hour (US$5 weekdays, US$7 weekends and holidays).

By Road from Macau It is possible to hire a car and guide from CTS (Macau) but most visitors join an organized tour.

By Boat from Hong Kong Jetcats (Hong Kong China Hydrofoil Co, Hong Kong, tel. 5-232136) make three trips a day from the Hong Kong China wharf to Jiuzhou in Zhuhai, a journey of 80 minutes (US$10 weekdays, US$10.25 weekends and holidays). Chu Kong Shipping (Hong Kong, tel. 3-671162) operates Jetcats from Kowloon and Hong Kong to Zhongshan harbour, close to Shiqi, four times a day (US$10).

By Air The CAAC helicopter fleet based in Zhuhai is currently on lease to the oil companies and not available to the public.

Tours It is possible to hire a car, driver and guide to tour Zhongshan independently (about HK$500 a day), but almost all foreign visitors join organized tours, which offer a variety of one-day and longer itineraries.

All one-day tours include visits to Zhuhai and the Sun Yatsen Memorial Park at Cuiheng. Some also take in Shiqi, the Zhongshan Hot Springs Resort, Longrui or a kindergarten. Lunch is served at Zhongshan, Cuiheng or the Zhongshan International Hotel in Shiqi. Most tours depart from Hong Kong early in the morning and return late afternoon, but some incorporate an overnight stay in Macau.

Overnight tours are available, using the Zhongshan International Hotel or the resorts at Zhongshan or Zhuhai. Zhongshan is also part of three- and four-day tours that continue on to Foshan and Canton before returning to Hong Kong.

These tours, and independent travel arrangements, are handled by CTS offices in Hong Kong and Macau and other agents, including International Tourism (143 Connaught Road, Hong Kong, tel. 5-412011; 9 Travessa do Pe. Narciso, Macau, tel. 86522), Macau Tours (287 Des Voeux Road, Hong Kong, tel. 5-422338; 9 Ave. da Amizade, Macau, tel. 855555), Sintra Tours (Shun Tak Centre, Hong Kong, tel. 5-408028; Sintra Hotel, Macau, tel. 86394), Macau Able (8 Connaught Road, Hong Kong, tel. 5-445656; 5 Travessa do Pe. Narciso, Macau, tel. 89798). Wah Nam Travel Service (Eastern Commercial Centre, 397 Hennessy Road, Hong Kong, tel. 5-8911161).

Prices have remained reasonable, thanks to the competition, and one-day tours are available from US$58, two-day itineraries from US$108 and three days from US$180, inclusive of transport from Hong Kong. Prices are slightly higher on weekends and holidays.

Hotels in Zhongshan and Zhuhai

In the last few years Zhongshan has experienced a hotel-building boom and the region now has accommodation of international standards at moderate rates. The Zhongshan International could compare favourably with hotels in Hong Kong, while the resorts combine modern facilities with revitalised late Qing design features, such as mustard-tiled roofed pavilions, carp pools, fountains, marble corridors and acres of ornate carvings and etched stained glass.

The rooms are airconditioned and have colour television which pick up Chinese and English programmes from Hong Kong. They have modern bathrooms and many now offer minibars and room service. Reservations are most easily made through travel agents in Hong Kong.

**Zhongshan
International Hotel**
2 Zhongshan Lu
Shiqi
tel. 24788
tlx. 44715
fax. 24736
cable 6662

中山国际酒店
石岐中山路 2 号

Fuhua Hotel
Sunwen Xi Lu
Shiqi
tel. 22034
tlx. 0294

富华酒店
石岐孙文西路

**Western Suburbs
Hotel (Xijiao
Binguan)**

西郊宾馆

**Zhongshan Hot
Springs Resort**
tel. 22811
tlx. 44828
cable 3306

中山温泉宾馆

*Double rooms US$28—36, suites from US$58
(20% discount weekdays, 5% weekends and
holidays)*

With 369 rooms in an impressive 20-storey
tower in the centre of Shiqi, this
CITS-operated hotel has a revolving
restaurant, Chinese and Western dining
rooms, a disco, pool and ornamental garden,
sauna, rooms for billiards and ten-pin
bowling, and rooms with all the facilities of an
international first-class property.

*Double rooms US$36; suites from US$58
(20% discount weekdays, 15% weekends and
holidays)*

This new 380-room hotel on the banks of the
river in Shiqi incorporates the former
Overseas Chinese Mansion and the
three-storey restaurant used by most
day-trippers in the past. The main tower has a
17-floor revolving restaurant, a vast marble
lobby, shopping arcades, a Chinese
restaurant, bar and exterior bubble elevator.
It also has the most interesting views in town,
of the river and pagoda hill.

Double rooms US$20

A budget hotel with 80 rooms in a round
tower close to the river, and Chinese and
Western restaurants.

*Double rooms US$22—9 weekdays, US$26—33
weekends and holidays (Hong Kong agent tel.
5-210377)*

The resort is 24 kilometres (15 miles) from
Macau, and 35 kilometres (22 miles) from
Shiqi. Occupying a vast area, the hotel has
Chinese and Western restaurants, pool, tennis
courts, horseback riding, shooting range,
shopping centre and nearby golf course (see
page 181). Built as a joint venture with

Sociedade de Turismo e Diversoes de Macau, it has 350 rooms in low-rise blocks, luxurious villas and 10-room bungalows, all with refrigerators, four with hot spring water baths.

Zhuhai Resort
Zhuhai
tel. 23718
tlx. 45618
cable 6333

珠海宾馆
珠海

Double rooms US$32—6; 2-bedroom villas US$179 (Macau agent tel. 552275)

Lavishly appointed and beautifully landscaped, this resort has gardens, ornamental pools, elegant villas, two pools, sauna, boating, tennis courts, dicso-conference centre, opulent Jade City Chinese restaurant and bar, waitresses in full-length, high-split skirts and brocade jackets. There are 200 rooms which are fairly basic but have stocked refrigerators.

Shijingshan Resort
Zhuhai
tel. 22393
cable 2828

石景山旅游中心
珠海

Double rooms US$29, 20% discount weekdays (Macau agent at Hotel Presidente tel. 553888 ext. 2104)

Next to the Zhuhai Resort, this was one of the first joint-venture hotels in China to open. It has two pools, boating, tennis courts, a shooting range and hillside garden of time-sculpted boulders. There are also good Chinese and Western restaurants and a large shopping centre. The 115 rooms are spread out in low-rise blocks and bungalows.

Cuiheng Hotel
Cuiheng Village
tel. 24091

翠亨宾馆
翠亨村

Double rooms US$29; cottages US$265, 20% discount weekdays

Located opposite the Sun Yatsen Memorial Park, this new hotel has a very attractive modern design, with 242 rooms in low-rise blocks and cottages, a pool and garden, Chinese and Western restaurants as well as a fully-equipped disco.

Gongbei Palace Hotel
Gongbei
tel. 86822

Double rooms US$27—36; villas US$85—92,10% discount weekdays

Situated close to the border with Macau, this

拱北宾馆
拱北

really looks like a Chinese palace, with swooping roofs of mustard-coloured tiles and rooms ranged around classical courtyards. It has 210 rooms, all with mini-bars, and villas with six rooms, plus a pool, Chinese and Western restaurants and a pleasant bar, sauna, shops and billiard room.

Changjiang Hotel
Changjiang Reservoir
tel. 23288
cable 0006

长江宾馆
长江水库

Double rooms US$26

This new 145-room hotel stands on the banks of the scenic Changjiang reservoir. It has Chinese and Western restaurants and meeting rooms all with superb views, of the reservoir, the landscaped garden or the rocky hillside behind the hotel which comprises a vertical garden of shrubs, pavilions and animal statues.

Restaurants in Zhongshan and Zhuhai

Zhongshan is one of the richest agricultural regions of Guangdong, with a wide variety of vegetable crops and fresh meat, fish and seafood, so it is only to be expected that eating out is generally a delight, even given the limits of set tourist meals offered on all tours. Typically these include chicken, fish, beef, pork, shrimp, soup, rice and lots of vegetables, with as much beer or soft drinks as required.

Most dishes are similar to those in Canton's restaurants (see page 61) but there are some local specialities. One is roast pigeon, with the small plump birds served crisp and tasty. Freshwater shrimps and carp are other regional favourites.

With the opening of new resorts and hotels, the quantity and often quality of restaurants have been greatly enhanced. It also means that there are now many good Western-style dining rooms, as well as a reasonable supply of Western wines and liquors.

Several of the new restaurants are as lavishly decorated as showcase Chinese restaurants in America or Europe. They feature carved wooden panelling, carpets, lanterns and furniture inspired by designs from the late 19th century, China's Victorian era. The opulent *chinoiserie* could not be more different from the standard post-revolutionary eating place — and the Chinese tourists love it.

One of the most gorgeous of these restaurants is the **Jade City** in the Zhuhai Hotel. It has mirrored ceiling vaults hung with bubble-lamp chandeliers, and windows of small coloured panes etched with pictures of birds, trees and landscapes. The furniture is of carved blackwood with plush upholstery. The waitresses wear full-length split-skirted cheongsams, and on the whole do justice to the slinky dress. The food fits the settings.

The **Kung Fu** in neighbouring Shijingshan Resort occupies two floors and looks like an imperial palace dining room. Here Chinese-tasselled lanterns and gilded decorations set the scene, and the food is excellent.

Some tour operators include lunches at these Zhuhai restaurants on their one-day tours, but most now seem to prefer the huge Chinese dining room in the **Zhongshan Hot Springs Hotel**, which is fast and efficient but no great culinary experience. Other one-day tours include lunch at the handsome restaurant at the **Cuiheng Hotel**, which has very good food, and a few opt for the **South China** restaurant in the **Gongbei Hotel**, an expensive first-class dining hall with palatial decor. Operators with longer itineraries offer superb meals at the elegant Chinese or French restaurants in the Zhongshan International Hotel or in the revolving restaurant of the Fuhua.

Sports and Entertainment

Zhongshan has become a playground for Chinese tourists, who flock to the big dippers, carousels, dodgems and boating ponds of Pearl Land and Changjiang. For Western visitors the great playing opportunities are two championship golf courses, at Zhongshan and Zhuhai. Both are brilliantly designed and offer facilities that rank with the best in Asia. The **Zhongshan Golf Club**, close to the Hot Springs Resort, was designed by Arnold Palmer's Course Design Company, and opened 1984. It is a 72-par, 5991-metre course of rolling hills, streams and tricky sand traps. The club house was designed by a Filipino company — the walls have rich wooden panelling, the furniture is high-grade rattan and the atmosphere is elegantly comfortable. Green fees are US$27 for 18 holes, US$32 for the whole of a weekday, and US$32 and US$38 on weekends and holidays. Caddies can be hired for US$6 per 18 holes and clubs are available for US$6. There is a resident pro and a pro shop and elegant spa. The club can be reached via Macau, or more directly via the jetcat service from Hong Kong to the Zhongshan wharf. Transport, transfers and reservations can be arranged by travel agents or through the club's office at 504 Pedder Building, 12 Pedder Street, Hong Kong, tel. 5-210377, tlx. 74040.

The **Zhuhai International Golf Club** was established by Japanese interests in 1985. It is located on the coast in Zhuhai, close to the

Macau border or Zhuhai ferry wharf. The 72-par, 6,380-metre course is wonderfully laid out in a long valley, with large sand traps, lakes and surrounding forests. The club house is a Japanese version of an ante-bellum mansion of the American south, with neo-classical columns and verandahs. It is attractively furnished and offers a restaurant, bar, pro shop and spa. Green fees are US$19 weekdays, US$32 weekends and holidays; caddies are US$5 and US$7.5, and rental of a set of clubs is US$10. In addition to individual arrangements golfers can buy a one-day package for US$36 weekdays, US$49 weekends, inclusive of transport from Hong Kong, or a two-day package for US$90 and US$102 with accommodation at Shijingshan. Prices include transport from Hong Kong. The agent is Zhuhai Tours, 3206 New World Tower, 16 Queen's Road Central, Hong Kong, tel. 5-232136. The club can be telephoned direct from Hong Kong (106) 8675624274.

Other than golf, there are plenty of tennis courts and most hotels have swimming pools. For evening entertainment, there are a few discos and occasional floor shows at hotel restaurants.

Sights in and around Zhongshan and Zhuhai

Cuiheng

Situated about 30 kilometres (19 miles) from Macau, and 29 kilometres (18 miles) from Shiqi, this is a national shrine to Sun Yatsen, the father of the 1911 revolution. Sun was born here in 1866 and in 1892 returned to build a house for his parents. Like some houses still to be found in Macau and Hong Kong the **Sun Yatsen Home** (Zhongshan Guju) combines Chinese and European features. The front has seven-arched verandahs along both storeys, and challenges ancient superstition by facing the 'unlucky' west. The interior is traditional, with high-ceilinged rooms, ancestral plaques, gilded carving and heavy, blackwood furniture including a Chinese roofed marriage bed. In the courtyard is the well of the original house and a silk tree planted by Sun with seeds from Hawaii.

Across the tree-shaded courtyard is the new **Sun Yatsen Museum**. The museum consists of light, airy rooms ranged around a patio, each showing the life and times of the man and the revolutionary hero. All labels are in Chinese, English and Japanese, and video displays playing in different parts of the museum have commentaries in all three languages. The museum is well worth an hour or more. Also in the memorial park is the Sun Yatsen Memorial High School, with blue-tiled roofs, which was built in 1934. It has about 700 students.

Dr Sun Yatsen

The man who is today probably the most revered modern Chinese hero, Sun Yatsen, was born in 1866 — appropriately the Year of the Tiger — in the village of Cuiheng (formerly written Tsui Hang), about 30 kilometres (19 miles) north of Macau, where his father once worked as a tailor. Like tens of thousands of young men from the area, Sun Yatsen sought his fortune overseas. At the age of 13 he sailed to Honolulu, where his elder brother had settled, and studied, first at the British Missionary School and later at Oahu College.

In 1883, when he was 17, he returned to his home village a changed person. He had been converted to Christianity and the ideals of western democracy, which he attempted to teach to the peasants of Zhongshan. This made him very unpopular with the local agents of the Manchu court, so he decided it would be better to continue his studies in Hong Kong.

He joined the faculty of medicine at Queen's College (later to become Hong Kong University) and in 1892 was one of the British colony's first Chinese graduates. That same year he was baptised into the Protestant church. His first medical post was in Macau, where he worked (without the necessary Portuguese licence) at the Kiang Vu hospital and his own clinic, where he treated the poor without pay. At the same time he wrote articles for the *Echo Macaense* advocating better education for the children of Zhongshan, help to the farmers and suppression of opium smoking.

The Manchu mandarins across the border recognized the rebel potential in Dr Sun, and put pressure on the Macau authorities to expel him. Sun decided to face the enemy head on and in 1894 went to Canton, where he set up a Revive China Society, aimed at forcing the Manchus to reform their rule in favour of the people. The Sino-Japanese war had just ended with China's humiliation, and some soldiers based in Canton mutinied because they had not been paid. The Society gave them support, which led the authorities to crush the mutiny and order Sun's arrest.

Sun evaded the police and escaped to Honolulu, whence he sent memorials to the Chinese court, demanding political reform. Then he sailed for London. In October 1896, in a bizarre plot which became headline news around the world, Sun was kidnapped in broad daylight and imprisoned in the Chinese Embassy. Spurred by Sun's former Hong Kong professor, Dr James Cantlie, the British press forced Parliament to demand his release.

Free again, Sun moved to Tokyo where he spent the next ten years organizing Chinese anti-Manchu exiles into revolutionary societies. Then he travelled through Europe and the United States to form similar societies and gather support and money from liberal Westerners. One American journalist described 'the presence of an unusually

self-possessed mind, as well as of a very strong character steeled against adversity.'

Sun's revolutionary programme stressed the need for 'giving free rein to people's talents and bringing agriculture into full play'. However, it was his call to overthrow the Manchu regime which became the priority of his followers in China. Their plans for an armed uprising in Wuhan were discovered by the authorities in the autumn of 1911, which forced the rebels to attack before Sun could get back from the United States.

By the time he reached China, the Manchu empire was no more. Sun was proclaimed 'Father of the Revolution' and named provisional president of the new republic. Meanwhile the country was reduced to political and economic chaos as revolutionary factions and opportunistic warlords battled for power.

Sun Yatsen was persuaded to retire in 1912 and reduced to a symbol and spokeman. For the last 13 years of his life he travelled around his war-torn country, preaching the ideals that had led to the revolution which now had no time for them.

Shiqi

The chief town of Zhongshan, formerly spelt Shekkei (based on the
name's pronunciation in Cantonese), has been an important market
centre and inland port for over 800 years. The town, which is 61
kilometres (38 miles) from Macau, and 79 kilometres (49 miles) from
Canton, has a population of about 100,000 and sits astride the busy Qi
River (Qijiang), where a cantilever bridge is opened mid-afternoon
and at midnight — or when a ship's captain pays for extra service. The
river is always interesting, with sampans, small freighters, ferries, and
floating restaurants (open until very late at night) moored along the
shore. Restaurants and night markets line the riverbank.

Symbol and landmark of the city is the Ming Dynasty pagoda, atop
the hill close to the heart of town, in a heavily wooded park where the
walkways are paved with Qing-Dynasty tomb stones. The pink and
white brick pagoda has an interior winding staircase, and at night is
garlanded with bands of red and green coloured lights.

Shiqi has much new construction, mostly of apartments, textile
factories and an impressive new hospital, in general financed by Hong
Kong Chinese. The most attractive is the **Sun Yatsen Memorial Hall**,
built for US$1.3 million by a Hong Kong construction tycoon in the
midtown park. Completed in 1983, it consists of a building with three
pagoda-shaped yellow-tiled towers. Inside is an auditorium with 1,400
seats for concerts and shows, and extensive exhibition halls. These
display Zhongshan's products, an excellent review of Sun Yatsen's life

and times (unfortunately only with Chinese captions), and a comprehensive survey of the emigration and achievements of Zhongshan Chinese overseas (by a rough estimation half a million now live in countries from Norway to Madagascar, California to Ghana and most places in between).

Many tours include a visit to one of Shiqi's kindergartens, where the children give a charming and photogenic song and dance show, and the guide details the government's school system.

For a one-time visit to China, Shiqi also offers a glimpse of the busy bicycle-packed streets and open-fronted stores.

Zhuhai

One of the four Special Economic Zones to be set up in 1980, Zhuhai was later extended to its present 14 square kilometres (5 square miles), including the town of Gongbei on the border with Macau. The population is about 150,000, with 30,000 in the chief town Xiangzhou. Zhuhai has proved one of the most successful SEZs with new factories producing textiles, medicine and electronic components for radios, televisions and sound equipment. The major industry, however, is tourism. Tens of thousands of Chinese, having paid their respects to Sun Yatsen, visit Zhuhai for a holiday at the glamorous new resorts and seaside funfairs. They also go on a shopping spree in the large, modern department stores crammed with goods from overseas and China. The most spectacular shopping centre is modelled on Beijing's imperial gates and stands between Zhuhai Hotel and Shijingshan Resort.

Chinese tourists see Zhuhai as a microcosm of Western luxury. There is, however, little evidence of traditional China as the building boom in holiday homes, office blocks and highways continues.

Zhuhai has its own international ferry pier and heliport, now used mostly by oil company employees.

Longrui

This small rural village is often visited on tours as an example of a farming community. This village used to be organized as a 'brigade', but in the early 80s the system of brigade, work units and communes was replaced by 'production responsibility', whereby farmers are taxed a proportion of their rice and sugarcane crops, and then are free to market privately any other produce. Longrui is a prosperous village which claims to produce 50 different crops. Visitors are welcomed into some of the farm houses, built in traditional style with stone floors, high ceilings and interconnecting rooms. All have courtyards, used for animals or storage. The village headquarters is a converted temple. The villagers number about 3,600 and proudly count 1,000 overseas residents in 17 countries.

Changjiang Reservoir

Located in the mountains south of Shiqi, the reservoir covers 300 square kilometres (116 square miles) and has a catchment area of 50,000 square kilometres (19,305 square miles). It is the largest reservoir in the county and provides water to Shiqi and surrounding areas. In recent years it has become a recreation centre with fairground rides, swimming pools, hotel rooms and villas.

Tower-house Villages

Seen from the tour bus as it speeds along the highway, they look like illusions. Why else should there be small European forts, complete with turrets, scattered among the paddy fields of Zhongshan? Unfortunately few tourists manage to get off the main roads to find out. If they did they would discover not only three- and four-storey fortresses, but small replicas of New York's Woolworth Building or buildings crowned with mock-Moorish domes and all manner of echoes of alien architecture.

Some Chinese guides maintain that they were built to protect the villages from bandits, which might have been one advantage, but the real source of the towers is part of the 19th-century emigrant story. Tens of thousands of young Chinese from Zhongshan left to make their fortune overseas and some of those who succeeded returned, and showed off their new affluence by building taller and fancier houses than their neighbours. Competition was keen and some of the villages have a veritable mini-Manhattan of highrises.

The most famous contest, however, was between two families who lived in nearby villages. The Kwok and the Ma clans each welcomed home a young man who had made good, and to celebrate they built some of the tallest towers in the county. In fact Mr Kwok and Mr Ma had done more than make good. They had created two of the biggest retail and trading empires in Asia — Wing On and Sincere — and, like Gimbels and Macy's, they continue to compete in Hong Kong.

Shenzhen

Shenzhen, across the border from Hong Kong, is the largest of China's Special Economic Zones. The zone was set up in 1979 to experiment with capitalism and to speed up the absorption of foreign funds. Tax concessions and other incentives are offered to encourage foreign investors and industrialists to participate in joint ventures. Enterprises based there now include electronics, textiles, clothing, food, furniture, printing, building materials and machinery. The city, which a few years ago had a population of 20,000, now has more than 330,000 people.

Shenzhen (or Shumchun, as it is spelt in Hong Kong) is sealed off from the rest of China, with its 84-kilometre (52.5-mile) border with Guangdong almost as closely guarded as its border with Hong Kong. Within the zone's 2,000 square kilometres (772 square miles), residents enjoy higher wages, easier access to consumer durables and a taste of Hong Kong-style entertainment.

Plans are going ahead to provide first-rate facilities, such as comprehensive commercial premises, an international airport and a large university campus. The Shenzhen skyline is already dominated by rows of skyscrapers, the tallest being the International Trading Conference Centre, which is topped with a revolving restaurant.

The city is still a sprawling mass of half-constructed tower blocks and half-made roads with little scenic interest for the foreign tourist. But for anyone interested in China's recent history, Shenzhen is well worth a visit. In scale alone, it is an extraordinary example of social and economic engineering.

Tourism is one of the most successful sectors of the zone's economy — the prime targets being Hong Kong residents who flock across the border to let off steam in the many resort hotels dotted around the attractive, hilly countryside. There are several large Disney-style amusement parks and water worlds as well as motor racing tracks and places where you can ride horses. At weekends and Hong Kong public holidays, hotels and transport get very crowded.

Shenzhen used to be popular with foreign travellers as the most inexpensive way of putting a foot in China on a day tour from Hong Kong. But as the zone's development progresses, and the whole of Guangdong Province becomes more accessible, its appeal is waning. CTS (HK) and some other Hong Kong tour operators run one-day tours which can be booked two days in advance in Hong Kong. Typically, these include a visit to one of the many reservoirs, to downtown shops, to a kindergarten or collective and to the Exhibition Hall at Shekou where some terracotta warriors from Xi'an can be seen, with lunch at a resort hotel. The tour cost is around US$49.

To the west of Shenzhen is the port of Shekou, also pursuing an ambitious development plan. Like Shenzhen, it is only recommended to those curious to see how China's Special Economic Zones are progressing.

Getting to Shenzhen

Visas to Shenzhen can be obtained at the border with Hong Kong. They cost US$6, and are valid for five days. Although the visa is for Shenzhen only, you may apply for a visa for the rest of China while in Shenzhen.

By Rail Trains to the Hong Kong border town of Lowu leave Hung Hom Railway Station in Kowloon every 20 minutes from 7.05 am onwards (US$2 one way). Immigration formalities take place at the border and take about half an hour. There are 14 trains a day to Shenzhen from Canton. The journey takes about two and a half hours. There is also one direct train a day between Shenzhen and Beijing, which takes about 56 hours.

By Road There is a daily service from Tsim Sha Tsui Ocean Terminal Bus Station in Kowloon to Honey Lake, passing through Shenzhen city, which leaves Hong Kong at 7.45 am and takes about two hours. Tickets can be purchased at any CTS office.

Minibuses bound for Shenzhen leave Canton throughout the day from outside the Liuhua Hotel. There are several airconditioned buses running between Shenzhen and Shantou, leaving early in the morning or, for overnight journeys, in the evening. The trip takes eight hours.

By Boat A jetfoil service from Hong Kong to Shekou leaves twice a day (at 8.10 am and 9.30 am) and takes 45 minutes (US$6 one way). Return services are at 2 pm and 4.20 pm. Tickets can be bought at China Travel Service (HK).

Getting around Shenzhen

There are plenty of taxis in the town. Minibuses, which leave from outside the railway station and collect passengers through the town, go to all the resorts and to Shekou.

CITS's main office is at 2 Chuanbu Jie, Heping Lu, tel. 38411, 38401, 22151. It has sub-offices in the railway station and on the second and third floors of the Customs Inspection Building, Lohu Port. It can help with hotel accommodation, transport and will also provide guide service.

Hotels in Shenzhen

International business-standard hotels

新都酒店 建设路
Century Plaza Hotel Jianshe Lu tel. 20888 tlx. 81320
(Hong Kong office tel. 5-8680638)

427 rooms. Double rooms US$49–83; suites US$103–385
Business centre, health club, swimming pool, Chinese and Western restaurants. Town-centre location. Managed by Hong Kong-based Pacifica Hotels International.

南海酒店 蛇口工业区
Nanhai Hotel Shekou Industrial Zone tel. 92888 tlx. 42879

400 rooms. Double rooms US$51–55; suites US$111–831
Business centre, health club, swimming pool, entertainment centre, shopping arcade. Waterfront location. Managed by Hong Kong-based Miramar Group.

雅园宾馆　东门路
Shenzhen International Hotel (Yayuan Binguan) Dongmen Lu
tel. 22763, 22773 tlx. 42299
(Hong Kong office tel. 3-7211555)

96 rooms. Double rooms US$40; suites US$66, US$103

上海宾馆　深南中路
Shenzhen Shanghai Hotel Shennan Zhong Lu tel. 41416

140 rooms. Double rooms US$22

西丽酒店　深南路
Xili Hotel Shennan Lu　tel. 60022

Opening 1987

Hotel resorts in Shenzhen

All these hotel resorts are located outside the city, by beaches,
reservoirs or the waterfront. Shuttle buses run to all of them, leaving
from outside the railway station every 20 minutes.

深圳湾大酒店　沙河
Shenzhen Bay Hotel Shahe tel. 70111 *(Hong Kong office tel. 3-693368)*

Double rooms US$40−2; suites US$128
Waterfront location (no beach), swimming pool, amusement park,
shops, disco, Chinese and Western food.

小梅沙海滨渡假村
Xiaomeisha Holiday Resort tel. 50000 *(Hong Kong office tel. 5-263383)*

Double rooms US$32 weekdays, US$42 weekends
Beach location.

香蜜湖渡假村
Honey Lake Hotel (Xiangmihu Dujiacun)

Double rooms US$31 weekdays, US$45 weekends
Western, Chinese and fast-food restaurants, amusement park, water
world, health centre, disco, horseriding, shops.

西丽湖渡假村
Xilihu Resort Hotel tel. 23711

Lakeside location. Rowing boats, horse riding and other recreational activities.

银湖旅游中心
Silver Lake Hotel (Yinhu Luyou Zhongxin) tel. 22727, 22834
tlx. 3-692811 *(Hong Kong office tel. 3-386111)*

Double rooms US$42
Valley reservoir location.

东湖宾馆
East Lake Hotel (Donghu Binguan) tel. 22727, 22728
(Hong Kong office tel. 5-8610504)

Double rooms US$28, US$42
Lake hill location.

明华客轮
Minghua Ocean Liner Shekou

This former cruise ship was built in France in 1962 and was purchased by China in 1973 to carry Chinese workers to Africa where they helped build the Tanzania-Zambia railway. She was later used for cruising operations out of Australia and has now retired as a floating 235-room hotel largely used by the domestic market.

Other hotels in Shenzhen

竹园宾馆　深惠公路
Bamboo Garden Hotel (Zhuyuan Binguan) Shenhui Gong Lu tel. 22911

Double rooms US$18−77

华侨大厦　和平路
Overseas Chinese Mansion (Huaqiao Dasha) Heping Lu tel. 22811

Double rooms US$17; dormitory US$4
Next to Shenzhen Railway Station. CTS has an office in the hotel.

Recommended Reading

Canton

Canton under Communism: Programs and Politics in a Provincial Capital 1949–68. Ezra Vogel (Harvard University Press)
Foreign Mud. Maurice Collis (Faber)
The Opium War Through Chinese Eyes. Arthur Waley (George Allen & Unwin)
Kwang Tung or Five Years in South China. J.A. Turner (Oxford University Press)
The 'Fan Kwae' at Canton, Before Treaty Days, 1825–1844. William C. Hunter (Kelly and Walsh)

China: Cultural Background

Anthology of Chinese Literature. Cyril Birch (Grove Press)
The Art and Architecture of China. Sickman & Soper (Penguin)
China: A Short Cultural History. C.P. Fitzgerald
Food in Chinese Culture. Ed. K.C. Chang (Yale University Press)
Nagel's Encyclopedia-guide to China
The Story of the Stone. Cao Xueqin, translated by D. Hawkes and John Minford (Penguin)
Seeds of Fire: Chinese Voices of Conscience. Edited by Geremie Barmé and John Minford (Far Eastern Economic Review)

China: History and Politics

The Gate of Heavenly Peace: the Chinese and Their Revolution, 1895–1980. Jonathan Spence (Penguin)
China Perceived: Images and Policies in Chinese-American Relations. J.K. Fairbank (Deutsch)
Communist China. Ed. Shurmann & Schell (Pelican)
Fanshen. William Hinton (Penguin)
Imperial China. Raymond Dawson (Hutchinson)
Imperial China. Ed. Shurmann & Schell (Pelican)
The Long March. Dick Wilson (Hamilton)
Mao and the Chinese Revolution. Jerome Ch'en (Oxford University Press)
Red Star over China. Edgar Snow (Gollancz)
The New Chinese Revolution. Lynn Pan (Hamish Hamilton)

Chronology of Periods in Chinese History

Palaeolithic	c.600,000−7000 BC
Neolithic	c.7000−1600 BC
Shang	c.1600−1027 BC
Western Zhou	1027−771 BC
Eastern Zhou	770−256 BC
Spring and Autumn	770−476 BC
Warring States	475−221 BC
Qin	221−207 BC
Western (Former) Han	206 BC−8 AD
Xin	9−24
Eastern (Later) Han	25−220
Three Kingdoms	220−265
Western Jin	265−316
Northern and Southern Dynasties	317−589
Sixteen Kingdoms	317−439
□Former Zhao	304−329
□Former Qin	351−383
□Later Qin	384−417
Northern Wei	386−534
Western Wei	535−556
Northern Zhou	557−581
Sui	581−618
Tang	618−907
Five Dynasties	907−960
Northern Song	960−1127
Southern Song	1127−1279
Jin (Jurchen)	1115−1234
Yuan (Mongol)	1279−1368
Ming	1368−1644
Qing (Manchu)	1644−1911
Republic	1911−1949
People's Republic	1949−

A Guide to Pronouncing Chinese Names

The official system of romanization used in China, which the visitor will find on maps, road signs and city shopfronts, is known as *Pinyin*. It is now almost universally adopted by the Western media.

Non-Chinese may initially encounter some difficulty in pronouncing romanized Chinese words. In fact many of the sounds correspond to the usual pronunciation of the letters in English. The exceptions are:

Initials

c	is like the *ts* in 'i*ts*'
q	is like the *ch* in '*ch*eese'
x	has no English equivalent, and can best be described as a hissing consonant that lies somewhere between *sh* and *s*. The sound was rendered as *hs* under an earlier transcription system.
z	is like the *ds* in 'fa*ds*'
zh	is unaspirated, and sounds like the *j* in '*j*ug'

Finals

a	sounds like 'ah'
e	is pronounced as in 'h*e*r'
i	is pronounced as in 'sk*i*' (written as *yi* when not preceded by an initial consonant). However, in *ci*, *chi*, *ri*, *shi*, *zi* and *zhi*, the sound represented by the *i* final is quite different and is similar to the *ir* in 's*ir*', but without much stressing of the *r* syllable.
o	sounds like the *aw* in 'l*aw*'
u	sounds like the *oo* in '*ooze*'
ê	is pronounced as in 'g*e*t'
ü	is pronounced as the German *ü* (written as *yu* when not preceded by an initial consonant)

The last two finals are usually written simply as *e* and *u*.

Finals in Combination

When two or more finals are combined, such as in *hao*, *jiao* and *liu*, each letter retains its sound value as indicated in the list above, but note the following:

ai	is like the *ie* in 't*ie*'
ei	is like the *ay* in 'b*ay*'
ian	is like the *ien* in 'V*ien*na'
ie	similar to 'ear'
ou	is like the *o* in 'c*o*de'
uai	sounds like 'why
uan	is like the *uan* in 'ig*uan*a' (except when preceded by *j*, *q*, *x* and *y*; in these cases a *u* following any of these four consonants is in fact *ü* and *uan* is similar to *uen*.)
ue	is like the *ue* in 'd*ue*t'
ui	sounds like 'way'

Examples

A few Chinese names are shown below with English phonetic spelling beside them:

Beijing	Bay-jing
Cixi	Tsi-shi
Guilin	Gway-lin
Hangzhou	Hahng-jo
Kangxi	Kahn-shi
Qianlong	Chien-lawng
Tiantai	Tien-tie
Xi'an	Shi-ahn

An apostrophe is used to separate syllables in certain compound-character words to preclude confusion. For example, *Changan* (which can be *chang-an* or *chan-gan*) is sometimes written as *Chang'an*.

Tones

A Chinese syllable consists of not only an initial and a final or finals, but also a tone or pitch of the voice when the words are spoken. In *Pinyin* the four basic tones are marked ‾, ´, ˇ and `. These marks are almost never shown in printed form except in language texts.

Useful Addresses

Canton

**China International Travel Service
Guangdong Branch**
Room 2366 Dongfang Hotel
tel. 669900 ext. 2366
中国国际旅行社广东分社　东方宾馆2366室

**China International Travel Service
Guangzhou Branch No 6 Reception Dept**
Room 2366 Dongfang Hotel
tel. 662427, 669900 ext. 2366
中国国际旅行社广州分社第六接待部
东方宾馆2366室

**China Travel Service
Guangdong Branch**
2 Qiaoguang Lu, Haizhu Guangchang
tel. 66112, 336888
tlx. 44217
cable 3307
广东省中国旅行社　海珠广场侨光路 2 号

Guangdong Tourism Service Corp
3rd Floor, 185 Huanshi Xi Lu
tel. 661610
广东旅游服务公司　环市西路185号 3 楼

**Guangdong Travel and Tourism General
Co**
185 Huanshi Xi Lu
tel. 662915, 661707, 663071
cable 4611
广东旅游总公司　环市西路185号

**Guangzhou Foreign Trade Centre
Travel Service Corp**
117 Liuhua Lu
tel. 332106
tlx. 44165
cable CECFA GUANGZHOU
中国(广州)对外贸易中心旅游服务公司
流花路117号

Guangzhou Travel Co
180 Huanshi Xi Lu
tel. 661515, 664574, 668800
tlx. 44575
cable 3394
广州市旅游公司　环市西路180号

**Civil Aviation Administration of China
(CAAC)
Guangdong Office**
181 Huanshi Lu
cable CAACCAN GUANGZHOU
Cargo
tel. 662917
International Passengers
tel. 661803
Domestic Passengers
tel. 662969
中国民航广州分局　环市路181号

CAAC Guangzhou Administration
Baiyun Airport
tel. 662123
中国民航广州管理局　白云机场

**China United Airlines
Ticketing Office**
113 Liuhua Lu
tel. 677739
中国联合航空公司售票处　流花路113号

**Guangzhou Civil Aviation Helicopter Co
Zhuhai Branch**
Zhuhai Heliport
tel. 20203, 22818, 22819
tlx. 45613
广州民航直升机公司珠海分公司
珠海特区直升机场

Guangzhou Harbour Passenger Station
Dashatou
tel. 333691
广州轮船客运站　大沙头

**Guangzhou Harbour Passenger Station
No 1 Pier**
Yangjiang Yi Lu
tel. 882874
广州轮船客运站 1 号码头　沿江一路

Guangzhou-Shenzhen Railway Corp
Guangzhou-Kowloon
Railway Station
tel. 664980
广深铁路公司　广九车站

Foshan

**China International Travel Service
Foshan Office**
64 Zumiao Lu
tel. 87923, 95775
中国国际旅行社佛山支社　祖庙路64号

**China Travel Service
Foshan Branch**
14 Zumiao Lu
tel. 86511
cable 4428
中国旅行社佛山分社　祖庙路14号

**China United Airlines
Ticketing Office**
9 Fenjiang Xi Lu
tel. 82255
中国联合航空公司售票处　汾江西路９号

Foshan Travel & Trading Co
105-7 Renmin Lu
tel. 85739
cable 1472
佛山市旅游贸易公司　人民路105-7号

Guilin

CAAC Guangxi Branch
144 Zhongshan Zhong Lu
tel. 3063, 5149
Guilin Airport
tel. 5118, 2832, 2826
Airport Information
tel. 2741
中国民航广西分局　中山中路144号

**China International Travel Service
Guilin Office**
14 Ronghu Bei Lu
tel. 2648
tlx. 48401
cable 0948
中国国际旅行社桂林支柱　榕湖北路14号

**China Travel Service
Guilin Office**
14 Ronghu Bei Lu
tel. 5395
tlx. 48463
cable 3535
中国旅行社桂林支柱　榕湖北路14号

**China United Airlines
Ticketing Office**
42 Nanhuan Lu
tel. 2152
中国联合航空公司售票处　南环路42号

Haikou

**China Travel Service of Hainan
Administrative Region**
17 Datong Lu
tel. 24523
tlx. 45039
cable 3307
中国旅行社海南分社　大同路17号

Haikou Travel and Tourism Co
15 Xinhua Bei Lu
tel. 24588
cable 2464
海口市旅游公司　新华北路15号

CAAC Haikou
50 Jiefang Lu
tel. 22515, 24614
中国民航　解放路50号

Hong Kong

CAAC Hong Kong
Ground Floor, Gloucester Tower
The Landmark, Central
tel. 5-215416
中国民航香港分局
置地广场告罗士打行地下

Chu Kong Shipping Company, Hong Kong
3 Shanghai Street, Kowloon
tel. 3-671162
珠江客运有限公司
九龙上海街３号地下

**Hong Kong and Yaumati Ferry Company,
Hong Kong**
2nd Floor, Central Harbour Service Pier
tel. 5-423081
香港油麻地小轮船有限公司
港内线码头２楼

Motor Transport Company of Guangdong and Hong Kong
152 Connaught Road Central
tel. 5-420871
43 Sai Yee Street, Kowloon
tel. 3-326002, 3-326091
粤港运输联营有限公司
香港干诺道中152号
九龙洗衣街43号

Shantou

China International Travel Service Shantou Branch
243 Wai Malu
tel. 75226
中国国际旅游服务公司汕头分社
外马路243号

China Travel Service Shantou Sub-Branch
Shanzhang Lu
tel. 33966, 33977
cable 3333
中国旅行社汕头分社　　汕樟路

Shantou SEZ Travel and Tourism Corp
Longhu District
Office
tel. 75090
Motorcade
tel. 75133
汕头经济特区旅游公司　　龙湖

Shantou Tourist General Co
86 Dahua Lu
tel. 75061
汕头旅游总公司　　大华路86号

Shantou Tourist Service Co
Yingchun Lu
tel. 73737
汕头旅游服务公司　　迎春路

China Ocean Shipping Shantou Agency Branch
10 Wai Malu
tel. 72853, 75977
cable PENAVICO SHANTOU
中国外轮代理汕头分公司　　外马路10号

CAAC Booking Shantou Office
46 Shanzhang Lu
tel. 32355
中国民航汕头售票处　　油樟路46号

Shenzhen

China International Travel Service Shenzhen Branch
2 Chuanbu Jie
Heping Lu
Manager's Office
tel. 38401
Room Reservation
tel. 22151
tlx. 42250
cable 1954
中国国际旅行社深圳分社
和平路船坞街 2 号

China Travel Service Shenzhen Branch
Yingchun Lu
tel. 39925
中国旅行社深圳分社　　迎春路

China United Airlines Ticketing Office
Friendship Hotel
3 Jiabin Lu
tel. 38280
中国联合航空公司售票处
嘉宾路 3 号友谊饭店

Shenzhen Special Zone Travel Agency
2 Baoping Jie, Heping Lu
tel. 38255, 27511, 27510
深圳经济特区旅游公司
和平路宝平街 2 号

Shenzhen Tourism Corp
9 Baoping Jie, Heping Lu
tel. 38326, 38412
cable 6664
深圳旅游公司　　和平路宝平街 9 号

Guangzhou-Shenzhen Railway Corp
75−1 Heping Lu
tel. 39684
广深铁路公司　　和平路75-1号

Shenzhen Airport
Nantouqu
tel. 23711 ext. 563
深圳机场　南头区

Shenzhen Bus Co
30 Hubei Lu
tel. 23497, 23552
深圳市公共汽车公司　湖贝路30号

Shenzhen Bus Station
53 Dongmen Lu
tel. 22465
深圳汽车站　东门路53号

China Merchants Steam Navigation Co Ltd
Shenzhen Office
Shenzhen
tel. 2449
招商局轮船深圳办事处　深圳

China Ocean Helicopter Corp
Room 201 Building No 111
Shangbu Lu, Yuanling Xincun
tel. 23293, 38427
tlx. 42210
cable 0237
中国海洋直升机专业公司
上埗路园岭新村111号201室

Zhanjiang

CAAC Zhanjiang
21 Renmin Dadao, Xiashan
tel. 24415
中国民航湛江分局　霞山人民大道21号

CAAC Zhanjiang Airfield
Xiashan Xincun
tel. 24345
湛江民航机场　霞山新村

CAAC Booking Zhanjiang Office
23 Renmin Yi Lu
tel. 24415
湛江民航售票处　人民一路23号

China Travel Service
Zhanjiang Branch
Renmin Lu
tel. 24966
cable 9918
中国旅行社湛江分社　人民路

China Ocean Helicopter Corp
Zhanjiang Branch
Potou Heliport
tel. 24100−2, 23111
tlx. 45245
中国海洋直升机专业公司湛江分公司
坡头直升机场

China Ocean Shipping Agency
Zhanjiang Branch
7 Renmin Dong Yi Lu
tel. 24936, 24497
tlx. 45234
cable PENAVICO ZHANJIANG
中国外轮代理公司湛江分公司
人民东一路7号

Zhanjiang Tours Co
Renmin Lu
tel. 23688, 24155
tlx. 45233
cable 8869
湛江旅游公司　人民路

Zhongshan

China International Travel Service
Zhongshan Office
Shiqi Xijiao
tel. 22243
fax. 24736
中国国际旅行社中山支社　石岐西郊

China Travel Service
Zhongshan Office
Sunwen Xi Lu, Shiqi
tel. 22034
cable 0294
中山市中国旅行社　石岐孙文西路

Zhuhai

China Travel Service
Gongbei Branch
Haibin Lu, Gongbei
tel. 85777
cable 3307
中国旅行社拱北分社　拱北海滨路

Shijingshan Tourist Centre
Jingshan Lu
tel. 22326, 22393, 23514
tlx. 45617
cable 2828
石景山旅游中心　景山路

Index of Places